MW00994993

FREE Test Taking Tips DVD Offer

To help us better serve you, we have developed a Test Taking Tips DVD that we would like to give you for FREE. **This DVD covers world-class test taking tips that you can use to be even more successful when you are taking your test.**

All that we ask is that you email us your feedback about your study guide. Please let us know what you thought about it – whether that is good, bad or indifferent.

To get your **FREE Test Taking Tips DVD**, email freedvd@studyguideteam.com with "FREE DVD" in the subject line and the following information in the body of the email:

    a. The title of your study guide.

    b. Your product rating on a scale of 1-5, with 5 being the highest rating.

    c. Your feedback about the study guide. What did you think of it?

    d. Your full name and shipping address to send your free DVD.

If you have any questions or concerns, please don't hesitate to contact us at freedvd@studyguideteam.com.

Thanks again!

SAT Literature Subject Test 2019 & 2020 Study Guide

Test Prep & Practice Test Questions for the College Board SAT Literature Subject Test

Test Prep Books

Table of Contents

Quick Overview

As you draw closer to taking your exam, effective preparation becomes more and more important. Thankfully, you have this study guide to help you get ready. Use this guide to help keep your studying on track and refer to it often.

This study guide contains several key sections that will help you be successful on your exam. The guide contains tips for what you should do the night before and the day of the test. Also included are test-taking tips. Knowing the right information is not always enough. Many well-prepared test takers struggle with exams. These tips will help equip you to accurately read, assess, and answer test questions.

A large part of the guide is devoted to showing you what content to expect on the exam and to helping you better understand that content. In this guide are practice test questions so that you can see how well you have grasped the content. Then, answer explanations are provided so that you can understand why you missed certain questions.

Don't try to cram the night before you take your exam. This is not a wise strategy for a few reasons. First, your retention of the information will be low. Your time would be better used by reviewing information you already know rather than trying to learn a lot of new information. Second, you will likely become stressed as you try to gain a large amount of knowledge in a short amount of time. Third, you will be depriving yourself of sleep. So be sure to go to bed at a reasonable time the night before. Being well-rested helps you focus and remain calm.

Be sure to eat a substantial breakfast the morning of the exam. If you are taking the exam in the afternoon, be sure to have a good lunch as well. Being hungry is distracting and can make it difficult to focus. You have hopefully spent lots of time preparing for the exam. Don't let an empty stomach get in the way of success!

When travelling to the testing center, leave earlier than needed. That way, you have a buffer in case you experience any delays. This will help you remain calm and will keep you from missing your appointment time at the testing center.

Be sure to pace yourself during the exam. Don't try to rush through the exam. There is no need to risk performing poorly on the exam just so you can leave the testing center early. Allow yourself to use all of the allotted time if needed.

Remain positive while taking the exam even if you feel like you are performing poorly. Thinking about the content you should have mastered will not help you perform better on the exam.

Once the exam is complete, take some time to relax. Even if you feel that you need to take the exam again, you will be well served by some down time before you begin studying again. It's often easier to convince yourself to study if you know that it will come with a reward!

Test-Taking Strategies

1. Predicting the Answer

When you feel confident in your preparation for a multiple-choice test, try predicting the answer before reading the answer choices. This is especially useful on questions that test objective factual knowledge or that ask you to fill in a blank. By predicting the answer before reading the available choices, you eliminate the possibility that you will be distracted or led astray by an incorrect answer choice. You will feel more confident in your selection if you read the question, predict the answer, and then find your prediction among the answer choices. After using this strategy, be sure to still read all of the answer choices carefully and completely. If you feel unprepared, you should not attempt to predict the answers. This would be a waste of time and an opportunity for your mind to wander in the wrong direction.

2. Reading the Whole Question

Too often, test takers scan a multiple-choice question, recognize a few familiar words, and immediately jump to the answer choices. Test authors are aware of this common impatience, and they will sometimes prey upon it. For instance, a test author might subtly turn the question into a negative, or he or she might redirect the focus of the question right at the end. The only way to avoid falling into these traps is to read the entirety of the question carefully before reading the answer choices.

3. Looking for Wrong Answers

Long and complicated multiple-choice questions can be intimidating. One way to simplify a difficult multiple-choice question is to eliminate all of the answer choices that are clearly wrong. In most sets of answers, there will be at least one selection that can be dismissed right away. If the test is administered on paper, the test taker could draw a line through it to indicate that it may be ignored; otherwise, the test taker will have to perform this operation mentally or on scratch paper. In either case, once the obviously incorrect answers have been eliminated, the remaining choices may be considered. Sometimes identifying the clearly wrong answers will give the test taker some information about the correct answer. For instance, if one of the remaining answer choices is a direct opposite of one of the eliminated answer choices, it may well be the correct answer. The opposite of obviously wrong is obviously right! Of course, this is not always the case. Some answers are obviously incorrect simply because they are irrelevant to the question being asked. Still, identifying and eliminating some incorrect answer choices is a good way to simplify a multiple-choice question.

4. Don't Overanalyze

Anxious test takers often overanalyze questions. When you are nervous, your brain will often run wild, causing you to make associations and discover clues that don't actually exist. If you feel that this may be a problem for you, do whatever you can to slow down during the test. Try taking a deep breath or counting to ten. As you read and consider the question, restrict yourself to the particular words used by the author. Avoid thought tangents about what the author *really* meant, or what he or she was *trying* to say. The only things that matter on a multiple-choice test are the words that are actually in the question. You must avoid reading too much into a multiple-choice question, or supposing that the writer meant something other than what he or she wrote.

5. No Need for Panic

It is wise to learn as many strategies as possible before taking a multiple-choice test, but it is likely that you will come across a few questions for which you simply don't know the answer. In this situation, avoid panicking. Because most multiple-choice tests include dozens of questions, the relative value of a single wrong answer is small. Moreover, your failure on one question has no effect on your success elsewhere on the test. As much as possible, you should compartmentalize each question on a multiple-choice test. In other words, you should not allow your feelings about one question to affect your success on the others. When you find a question that you either don't understand or don't know how to answer, just take a deep breath and do your best. Read the entire question slowly and carefully. Try rephrasing the question a couple of different ways. Then, read all of the answer choices carefully. After eliminating obviously wrong answers, make a selection and move on to the next question.

6. Confusing Answer Choices

When working on a difficult multiple-choice question, there may be a tendency to focus on the answer choices that are the easiest to understand. Many people, whether consciously or not, gravitate to the answer choices that require the least concentration, knowledge, and memory. This is a mistake. When you come across an answer choice that is confusing, you should give it extra attention. A question might be confusing because you do not know the subject matter to which it refers. If this is the case, don't eliminate the answer before you have affirmatively settled on another. When you come across an answer choice of this type, set it aside as you look at the remaining choices. If you can confidently assert that one of the other choices is correct, you can leave the confusing answer aside. Otherwise, you will need to take a moment to try to better understand the confusing answer choice. Rephrasing is one way to tease out the sense of a confusing answer choice.

7. Your First Instinct

Many people struggle with multiple-choice tests because they overthink the questions. If you have studied sufficiently for the test, you should be prepared to trust your first instinct once you have carefully and completely read the question and all of the answer choices. There is a great deal of research suggesting that the mind can come to the correct conclusion very quickly once it has obtained all of the relevant information. At times, it may seem to you as if your intuition is working faster even than your reasoning mind. This may in fact be true. The knowledge you obtain while studying may be retrieved from your subconscious before you have a chance to work out the associations that support it. Verify your instinct by working out the reasons that it should be trusted.

8. Key Words

Many test takers struggle with multiple-choice questions because they have poor reading comprehension skills. Quickly reading and understanding a multiple-choice question requires a mixture of skill and experience. To help with this, try jotting down a few key words and phrases on a piece of scrap paper. Doing this concentrates the process of reading and forces the mind to weigh the relative importance of the question's parts. In selecting words and phrases to write down, the test taker thinks about the question more deeply and carefully. This is especially true for multiple-choice questions that are preceded by a long prompt.

9. Subtle Negatives

One of the oldest tricks in the multiple-choice test writer's book is to subtly reverse the meaning of a question with a word like *not* or *except*. If you are not paying attention to each word in the question, you can easily be led astray by this trick. For instance, a common question format is, "Which of the following is…?" Obviously, if the question instead is, "Which of the following is not…?," then the answer will be quite different. Even worse, the test makers are aware of the potential for this mistake and will include one answer choice that would be correct if the question were not negated or reversed. A test taker who misses the reversal will find what he or she believes to be a correct answer and will be so confident that he or she will fail to reread the question and discover the original error. The only way to avoid this is to practice a wide variety of multiple-choice questions and to pay close attention to each and every word.

10. Reading Every Answer Choice

It may seem obvious, but you should always read every one of the answer choices! Too many test takers fall into the habit of scanning the question and assuming that they understand the question because they recognize a few key words. From there, they pick the first answer choice that answers the question they believe they have read. Test takers who read all of the answer choices might discover that one of the latter answer choices is actually *more* correct. Moreover, reading all of the answer choices can remind you of facts related to the question that can help you arrive at the correct answer. Sometimes, a misstatement or incorrect detail in one of the latter answer choices will trigger your memory of the subject and will enable you to find the right answer. Failing to read all of the answer choices is like not reading all of the items on a restaurant menu: you might miss out on the perfect choice.

11. Spot the Hedges

One of the keys to success on multiple-choice tests is paying close attention to every word. This is never more true than with words like *almost*, *most*, *some*, and *sometimes*. These words are called "hedges" because they indicate that a statement is not totally true or not true in every place and time. An absolute statement will contain no hedges, but in many subjects, like literature and history, the answers are not always straightforward or absolute. There are always exceptions to the rules in these subjects. For this reason, you should favor those multiple-choice questions that contain hedging language. The presence of qualifying words indicates that the author is taking special care with his or her words, which is certainly important when composing the right answer. After all, there are many ways to be wrong, but there is only one way to be right! For this reason, it is wise to avoid answers that are absolute when taking a multiple-choice test. An absolute answer is one that says things are either all one way or all another. They often include words like *every*, *always*, *best*, and *never*. If you are taking a multiple-choice test in a subject that doesn't lend itself to absolute answers, be on your guard if you see any of these words.

12. Long Answers

In many subject areas, the answers are not simple. As already mentioned, the right answer often requires hedges. Another common feature of the answers to a complex or subjective question are qualifying clauses, which are groups of words that subtly modify the meaning of the sentence. If the question or answer choice describes a rule to which there are exceptions or the subject matter is complicated, ambiguous, or confusing, the correct answer will require many words in order to be expressed clearly and accurately. In essence, you should not be deterred by answer choices that seem excessively long. Oftentimes, the author of the text will not be able to write the correct answer without offering some qualifications and modifications. Your job is to read the answer choices thoroughly and completely and to select the one that most accurately and precisely answers the question.

13. Restating to Understand

Sometimes, a question on a multiple-choice test is difficult not because of what it asks but because of how it is written. If this is the case, restate the question or answer choice in different words. This process serves a couple of important purposes. First, it forces you to concentrate on the core of the question. In order to rephrase the question accurately, you have to understand it well. Rephrasing the question will concentrate your mind on the key words and ideas. Second, it will present the information to your mind in a fresh way. This process may trigger your memory and render some useful scrap of information picked up while studying.

14. True Statements

Sometimes an answer choice will be true in itself, but it does not answer the question. This is one of the main reasons why it is essential to read the question carefully and completely before proceeding to the answer choices. Too often, test takers skip ahead to the answer choices and look for true statements. Having found one of these, they are content to select it without reference to the question above. Obviously, this provides an easy way for test makers to play tricks. The savvy test taker will always read the entire question before turning to the answer choices. Then, having settled on a correct answer choice, he or she will refer to the original question and ensure that the selected answer is relevant. The mistake of choosing a correct-but-irrelevant answer choice is especially common on questions related to specific pieces of objective knowledge, like historical or scientific facts. A prepared test taker will have a wealth of factual knowledge at his or her disposal, and should not be careless in its application.

15. No Patterns

One of the more dangerous ideas that circulates about multiple-choice tests is that the correct answers tend to fall into patterns. These erroneous ideas range from a belief that B and C are the most common right answers, to the idea that an unprepared test-taker should answer "A-B-A-C-A-D-A-B-A." It cannot be emphasized enough that pattern-seeking of this type is exactly the WRONG way to approach a multiple-choice test. To begin with, it is highly unlikely that the test maker will plot the correct answers according to some predetermined pattern. The questions are scrambled and delivered in a random order. Furthermore, even if the test maker was following a pattern in the assignation of correct answers, there is no reason why the test taker would know which pattern he or she was using. Any attempt to discern a pattern in the answer choices is a waste of time and a distraction from the real work of taking the test. A test taker would be much better served by extra preparation before the test than by reliance on a pattern in the answers.

FREE DVD OFFER

Don't forget that doing well on your exam includes both understanding the test content and understanding how to use what you know to do well on the test. We offer a completely FREE Test Taking Tips DVD that covers world class test taking tips that you can use to be even more successful when you are taking your test.

All that we ask is that you email us your feedback about your study guide. To get your **FREE Test Taking Tips DVD**, email freedvd@studyguideteam.com with "FREE DVD" in the subject line and the following information in the body of the email:

The title of your study guide.
Your product rating on a scale of 1-5, with 5 being the highest rating.
Your feedback about the study guide. What did you think of it?
Your full name and shipping address to send your free DVD.

Introduction

Function of the Test

The SAT Subject Test in Literature is required by many colleges in the U.S. for students who are looking to attend college and showcase their interests in English or creative writing. Some colleges use the SAT Subject Test in Literature to place students in appropriate courses in college, allowing them to pass over the basics into more complex courses. Note that in New York State, some people may use SAT Subject Test scores as a substitute for a Regents examination score. It's recommended that test takers have knowledge of three or four years of literary study, experience in critically reading American and English literature from various historical periods, and an extensive knowledge of novels, plays, poetry, and prose.

Test Administration

To find out where the SAT Subject Test in Literature is given, go to the website at collegereadiness.collegeboard.org. There you can find exam dates for the current year as well as up to three years in advance. The dates are listed by subject and give a deadline to register for each date. Currently, there are six dates listed each year for taking the subject tests, all of which offer the literature subject test. The dates for the exams are offered in August, October, November, December, May, and June. Note that you cannot take the SAT and an SAT Subject Test on the same date. The College Board website also has a test date finder, where you enter in the test date and your country, state, and city. The results bring up testing centers in your area or the area(s) nearest you.

Test Format

The SAT Literature Subject test is sixty minutes long and has sixty multiple choice questions. The test has six to eight passages with several questions based on each passage. The passages may not list the author, but they are usually followed by a date of first publication. Because of the wide range of literary texts available to students in various academic setting and the limited amount of questions on the test, test-takers should not expect to know every genre, author, or text given. Although some questions do ask about authorship, genre, or historical context, many questions focus on how well you read the passage and analysis of that passage.

The test content is divided into three separate categories: source of questions, chronology, and genre. The source of questions come from American literature (40 to 50%), English literature (40 to 50%), and other literature written in English (0 to 10%). Chronology question come from the Renaissance and 17th century (30%), the 18th and 19th centuries (30%), and the 20th century (40%). Finally, there are 40 to 50% of prose passages, 40 to 50% of poetry passages, and 0 to 10% of drama and other passages.

Test takers who are preparing for the SAT Subject Test in Literature will want to know basic literary terminology, such as point-of-view, alliteration, irony, stanza, tone, character, and image. Understanding of literary concepts such as theme, use of language, form and organization, narrative voice, and characterization are also important.

Scoring

In 2016, 57,761 students took the SAT Subject Test in Literature. Out of a 200 to 800-point scale, the mean score was 599. The standard deviation on the literature test was 122; this calculates the spread of grades around the average score. A "good score" for the subject test in literature depends on the college you are applying to. Although many colleges are flexible and look at SAT scores along with other factors for admissions, the average number many colleges like to see on the literature test is a score of 650 or above. For more selective schools, the request for a score of 700 or 750 and above is more prevalent.

Recent Developments

March testing is available internationally, and subject tests will be offered outside of the U.S. and U.S. territories in October, November, December, May, and June.

Literary Terms and Concepts

Figurative Language

Literary texts also employ rhetorical devices. Figurative language like simile and metaphor is a type of rhetorical device commonly found in literature. In addition to rhetorical devices that play on the *meanings* of words, there are also rhetorical devices that use the *sounds* of words. These devices are most often found in poetry but may also be found in other types of literature and in non-fiction writing like speech texts.

Alliteration and assonance are both varieties of sound repetition. Other types of sound repetition include: anaphora, repetition that occurs at the beginning of the sentences; epiphora, repetition occurring at the end of phrases; antimetabole, repetition of words in reverse order; and antiphrasis, a form of denial of an assertion in a text.

Alliteration refers to the repetition of the first sound of each word. Recall Robert Burns' opening line:

> My love is like a red, red rose

This line includes two instances of alliteration: "love" and "like" (repeated *L* sound), as well as "red" and "rose" (repeated *R* sound). Next, assonance refers to the repetition of vowel sounds, and can occur anywhere within a word (not just the opening sound). Here is the opening of a poem by John Keats:

> When I have fears that I may cease to be
>
> Before my pen has glean'd my teeming brain

Assonance can be found in the words "fears," "cease," "be," "glean'd," and "teeming," all of which stress the long *E* sound. Both alliteration and assonance create a harmony that unifies the writer's language.

Another sound device is **onomatopoeia**, or words whose spelling mimics the sound they describe. Words like "crash," "bang," and "sizzle" are all examples of onomatopoeia. Use of onomatopoetic language adds auditory imagery to the text.

Readers are probably most familiar with the technique of **pun**. A pun is a play on words, taking advantage of two words that have the same or similar pronunciation. Puns can be found throughout Shakespeare's plays, for instance:

> Now is the winter of our discontent
>
> Made glorious summer by this son of York

These lines from *Richard III* contain a play on words. Richard III refers to his brother, the newly crowned King Edward IV, as the "son of York," referencing their family heritage from the house of York. However, while drawing a comparison between the political climate and the weather (times of political trouble were the "winter," but now the new king brings "glorious summer"), Richard's use of the word "son" also implies another word with the same pronunciation, "sun"—so Edward IV is also like the sun, bringing light, warmth, and hope to England. Puns are a clever way for writers to suggest two meanings at once.

Some examples of figurative language are included in the following graphic.

	Definition	Example
Simile	Compares two things using "like" or "as"	Her hair was like gold.
Metaphor	Compares two things as if they are the same	He was a giant teddy bear.
Idiom	Using words with predictable meanings to create a phrase with a different meaning	The world is your oyster.
Alliteration	Repeating the same beginning sound or letter in a phrase for emphasis	The busy baby babbled.
Personification	Attributing human characteristics to an object or an animal	The house glowered menacingly with a dark smile.
Foreshadowing	Giving an indication that something is going to happen later in the story	I wasn't aware at the time, but I would come to regret those words.
Symbolism	Using symbols to represent ideas and provide a different meaning	The ring represented the bond between us.
Onomatopoeia	Using words that imitate sound	The tire went off with a bang and a crunch.
Imagery	Appealing to the senses by using descriptive language	The sky was painted with red and pink and streaked with orange.
Hyperbole	Using exaggeration not meant to be taken literally	The girl weighed less than a feather.

Figurative language can be used to give additional insight into the theme or message of a text by moving beyond the usual and literal meaning of words and phrases. It can also be used to appeal to the senses of readers and create a more in-depth story.

Counterarguments and Evaluating Arguments

If an author presents a differing opinion or a counterargument in order to refute it, the reader should consider how and why this information is being presented. It is meant to strengthen the original argument and shouldn't be confused with the author's intended conclusion, but it should also be considered in the reader's final evaluation.

Authors can also use bias if they ignore the opposing viewpoint or present their side in an unbalanced way. A strong argument considers the opposition and finds a way to refute it. Critical readers should look for an unfair or one-sided presentation of the argument and be skeptical, as a bias may be present. Even if this bias is unintentional, if it exists in the writing, the reader should be wary of the validity of the argument. Readers should also look for the use of stereotypes, which refer to specific groups. Stereotypes are often negative connotations about a person or place, and should always be avoided.

When a critical reader finds stereotypes in a piece of writing, they should be critical of the argument, and consider the validity of anything the author presents. Stereotypes reveal a flaw in the writer's thinking and may suggest a lack of knowledge or understanding about the subject.

In general, readers should always heed attention to whether an author's ideas or stated facts are relevant to the argument or counterargument posed in the reading. Those that are irrelevant can cloud the argument or weaken it. In much the same way, critical readers are able to identify whether statements in a reading strengthen or weaken the author's argument.

Authors want you to accept their assertions and arguments as true but critical readers evaluate the strength of the argument instead of simply taking it at face value and accepting it as the truth or only point of view. All arguments need two parts: the claim and the supporting evidence or rationale. The claim *is* the argument. It asserts an opinion, idea, point of view, or conclusion. The supporting evidence is the rationale, assumptions, beliefs, as well as the factual evidence in support of the stated claim. The supporting evidence is what gives readers the information necessary to accept or reject the stated claim. Critical readers should assess the argument in its entirety by evaluating the claims and conclusions themselves, the process of reasoning, and the accuracy of the evidence. For example, arguments are weaker and should be skeptically considered when the supporting evidence is highly opinionated, biased, or derived from sources that are not credible. Authors should cite where statistics and other stated facts were found. Lastly, the support for a claim should be pertinent to it and consistent with the other statements and evidence.

Opinions, Facts, and Fallacies

As mentioned previously, authors write with a purpose. They adjust their writing for an intended audience. It is the readers' responsibility to comprehend the writing style or purpose of the author. When readers understand a writer's purpose, they can then form their own thoughts about the text(s) regardless of whether their thoughts are the same as or different from the author's. The following section will examine different writing tactics that authors use, such as facts versus opinions, bias and stereotypes, appealing to the readers' emotions, and fallacies (including false analogies, circular reasoning, false dichotomy, and overgeneralization).

Facts Versus Opinions
Readers need to be aware of the writer's purpose to help discern facts and opinions within texts. A **fact** is a piece of information that is true. It can either prove or disprove claims or arguments presented in texts. Facts cannot be changed or altered. For example, the statement: *Abraham Lincoln was assassinated on April 15, 1865*, is a fact. The date and related events cannot be altered.

Authors not only present facts in their writing to support or disprove their claim(s), but they may also express their opinions. Authors may use facts to support their own opinions, especially in a persuasive text; however, that does not make their opinions facts. An **opinion** is a belief or view formed about something that is not necessarily based on the truth. Opinions often express authors' personal feelings about a subject and use words like *believe, think,* or *feel. For example, the statement: *Abraham Lincoln was the best president who has ever lived*, expresses the writer's opinion. Not all writers or readers agree or disagree with the statement. Therefore, the statement can be altered or adjusted to express opposing or supporting beliefs, such as "Abraham Lincoln was the worst president who has ever lived" or "I also think Abraham Lincoln was a great president."

When authors include facts and opinions in their writing, readers may be less influenced by the text(s). Readers need to be conscious of the distinction between facts and opinions while going through texts.

Not only should the intended audience be vigilant in following authors' thoughts versus valid information, readers need to check the source of the facts presented. Facts should have reliable sources derived from credible outlets like almanacs, encyclopedias, medical journals, and so on.

Bias and Stereotypes

Not only can authors state facts or opinions in their writing, they sometimes intentionally or unintentionally show bias or portray a stereotype. A **bias** is when someone demonstrates a prejudice in favor of or against something or someone in an unfair manner. When an author is biased in his or her writing, readers should be skeptical despite the fact that the author's bias may be correct. For example, two athletes competed for the same position. One athlete is related to the coach and is a mediocre athlete, while the other player excels and deserves the position. The coach chose the less talented player who is related to him for the position. This is a biased decision because it favors someone in an unfair way.

Similar to a bias, a **stereotype** shows favoritism or opposition but toward a specific group or place. Stereotypes create an oversimplified or overgeneralized idea about a certain group, person, or place. For example,

>   Women are horrible drivers.

This statement basically labels *all* women as horrible drivers. While there may be some terrible female drivers, the stereotype implies that *all* women are bad drivers when, in fact, not *all* women are. While many readers are aware of several vile ethnic, religious, and cultural stereotypes, audiences should be cautious of authors' flawed assumptions because they can be less obvious than the despicable examples that are unfortunately pervasive in society.

Overall Meaning

Identifying Theme or Central Message

In literature, a theme can often be determined by considering the over-arching narrative conflict within the work. Though there are several types of conflicts and several potential themes within them, the following are the most common:

- *Individual against the self*—relevant to themes of self-awareness, internal struggles, pride, coming of age, facing reality, fate, free will, vanity, loss of innocence, loneliness, isolation, fulfillment, failure, and disillusionment

- *Individual against nature*—relevant to themes of knowledge vs. ignorance, nature as beauty, quest for discovery, self-preservation, chaos and order, circle of life, death, and destruction of beauty

- *Individual against society*—relevant to themes of power, beauty, good, evil, war, class struggle, totalitarianism, role of men/women, wealth, corruption, change vs. tradition, capitalism, destruction, heroism, injustice, and racism

- *Individual against another individual*—relevant to themes of hope, loss of love or hope, sacrifice, power, revenge, betrayal, and honor

For example, in Hawthorne's *The Scarlet Letter*, one possible narrative conflict could be the individual against the self, with a relevant theme of internal struggles. This theme is alluded to through characterization—Dimmesdale's moral struggle with his love for Hester and Hester's internal struggles with the truth and her daughter, Pearl. It's also alluded to through plot—Dimmesdale's suicide and Hester helping the very townspeople who initially condemned her.

Sometimes, a text can convey a **message** or universal lesson—a truth or insight that the reader infers from the text, based on analysis of the literary and/or poetic elements. This message is often presented as a statement. For example, a potential message in Shakespeare's *Hamlet* could be "Revenge is what ultimately drives the human soul." This message can be immediately determined through plot and characterization in numerous ways, but it can also be determined through the setting of Norway, which is bordering on war.

How Authors Develop Theme

Authors employ a variety of techniques to present a theme. They may compare or contrast characters, events, places, ideas, or historical or invented settings to speak thematically. They may use analogies, metaphors, similes, allusions, or other literary devices to convey the theme. An author's use of diction, syntax, and tone can also help convey the theme. Authors will often develop themes through the development of characters, use of the setting, repetition of ideas, use of symbols, and through contrasting value systems. Authors of both fiction and nonfiction genres will use a variety of these techniques to develop one or more themes.

Regardless of the literary genre, there are commonalities in how authors, playwrights, and poets develop themes or central ideas.

Authors often do research, the results of which contributes to theme. In prose fiction and drama, this research may include real historical information about the setting the author has chosen or include elements that make fictional characters, settings, and plots seem realistic to the reader. In nonfiction, research is critical since the information contained within this literature must be accurate and, moreover, accurately represented.

In fiction, authors present a narrative conflict that will contribute to the overall theme. In fiction, this conflict may involve the storyline itself and some trouble within characters that needs resolution. In nonfiction, this conflict may be an explanation or commentary on factual people and events.

Authors will sometimes use character motivation to convey theme, such as in the example from *Hamlet* regarding revenge. In fiction, the characters an author creates will think, speak, and act in ways that effectively convey the theme to readers. In nonfiction, the characters are factual, as in a biography, but authors pay particular attention to presenting those motivations to make them clear to readers.

Authors also use literary devices as a means of conveying theme. For example, the use of moon symbolism in Shelley's *Frankenstein* is significant as its phases can be compared to the phases that the Creature undergoes as he struggles with his identity.

The selected point of view can also contribute to a work's theme. The use of first person point of view in a fiction or non-fiction work engages the reader's response differently than third person point of view. The central idea or theme from a first-person narrative may differ from a third-person limited text.

In literary nonfiction, authors usually identify the purpose of their writing, which differs from fiction, where the general purpose is to entertain. The purpose of nonfiction is usually to inform, persuade, or entertain the audience. The stated purpose of a non-fiction text will drive how the central message or theme, if applicable, is presented.

Authors identify an audience for their writing, which is critical in shaping the theme of the work. For example, the audience for J.K. Rowling's *Harry Potter* series would be different than the audience for a biography of George Washington. The audience an author chooses to address is closely tied to the purpose of the work. The choice of an audience also drives the choice of language and level of diction an author uses. Ultimately, the intended audience determines the level to which that subject matter is presented and the complexity of the theme.

Form

Text Structure
Depending on what the author is attempting to accomplish, certain formats or text structures work better than others. For example, a sequence structure might work for narration but not when identifying similarities and differences between dissimilar concepts. Similarly, a comparison-contrast structure is not useful for narration. It's the author's job to put the right information in the correct format.

Readers should be familiar with the five main literary structures:

1. **Sequence** structure (sometimes referred to as the order structure) is when the order of events proceed in a predictable order. In many cases, this means the text goes through the plot elements: exposition, rising action, climax, falling action, and resolution. Readers are introduced to characters, setting, and conflict in the exposition. In the rising action, there's an increase in tension and suspense. The climax is the height of tension and the point of no return. Tension decreases during the falling action. In the resolution, any conflicts presented in the exposition are solved, and the story concludes. An informative text that is structured sequentially will often go in order from one step to the next.

2. In the **problem-solution** structure, authors identify a potential problem and suggest a solution. This form of writing is usually divided into two paragraphs and can be found in informational texts. For example, cell phone, cable and satellite providers use this structure in manuals to help customers troubleshoot or identify problems with services or products.

3. When authors want to discuss similarities and differences between separate concepts, they arrange thoughts in a **comparison-contrast** paragraph structure. Venn diagrams are an effective graphic organizer for comparison-contrast structures, because they feature two overlapping circles that can be used to organize similarities and differences. A comparison-contrast essay organizes one paragraph based on similarities and another based on differences. A comparison-contrast essay can also be arranged with the similarities and differences of individual traits addressed within individual paragraphs. Words such as *however*, *but*, and *nevertheless* help signal a contrast in ideas.

4. **Descriptive** writing structure is designed to appeal to your senses. Much like an artist who constructs a painting, good descriptive writing builds an image in the reader's mind by appealing to the five senses: sight, hearing, taste, touch, and smell. However, overly descriptive writing can become tedious; sparse descriptions can make settings and characters seem flat. Good authors strike a balance by applying descriptions only to passages, characters, and settings that are integral to the plot.

5. Passages that use the **cause and effect** structure are simply asking *why* by demonstrating some type of connection between ideas. Words such as *if, since, because, then,* or *consequently* indicate relationship. By switching the order of a complex sentence, the writer can rearrange the emphasis on different clauses. Saying *If Sheryl is late, we'll miss the dance* is different from saying *We'll miss the dance if Sheryl is late*. One emphasizes Sheryl's tardiness while the other emphasizes missing the dance.

Paragraphs can also be arranged in a cause and effect format. Since the format—before and after—is sequential, it is useful when authors wish to discuss the impact of choices. Researchers often apply this paragraph structure to the scientific method.

<u>Types of Writing</u>
Writing can be classified under four passage types: narrative, expository, descriptive (sometimes called technical), and persuasive. Though these types are not mutually exclusive, one form tends to dominate the rest. By recognizing the *type* of passage you're reading, you gain insight into *how* you should read. If you're reading a narrative, you can assume the author intends to entertain, which means you may skim the text without losing meaning. A technical document might require a close read, because skimming the passage might cause the reader to miss salient details.

1. **Narrative** writing, at its core, is the art of storytelling. For a narrative to exist, certain elements must be present. It must have characters. While many characters are human, characters could be defined as anything that thinks, acts, and talks like a human. For example, many recent movies, such as *Lord of the Rings* and *The Chronicles of Narnia*, include animals, fantastical creatures, and even trees that behave like humans. It must have a plot or sequence of events. Typically, those events follow a standard plot diagram, but recent trends start *in medias res* or in the middle (near the climax). In this instance, foreshadowing and flashbacks often fill in plot details. Along with characters and a plot, there must also be conflict. Conflict is usually divided into two types: internal and external. Internal conflict indicates the character is in turmoil. Internal conflicts are presented through the character's thoughts. External conflicts are visible. Types of external conflict include a person versus nature, another person, and society.

2. **Expository writing** is detached and to the point. Since expository writing is designed to instruct or inform, it usually involves directions and steps written in second person ("you" voice) and lacks any persuasive or narrative elements. **Sequence words** such as first, second, and third, or in the first place, secondly, and lastly are often given to add fluency and cohesion. Common examples of expository writing include instructor's lessons, cookbook recipes, and repair manuals.

3. Due to its empirical nature, **technical** writing is filled with steps, charts, graphs, data, and statistics. The goal of technical writing is to advance understanding in a field through the scientific method. Experts such as teachers, doctors, or mechanics use words unique to the profession in which they operate. These words, which often incorporate acronyms, are called **jargon**. Technical writing is a type of expository writing but is not meant to be understood by the general public. Instead, technical writers assume readers have received a formal education in a particular field of study and need no explanation as to what the jargon means. Imagine a doctor trying to understand a diagnostic reading for a car or a mechanic trying to interpret lab results. Only professionals with proper training will fully comprehend the text.

4. **Persuasive** writing is designed to change opinions and attitudes. The topic, stance, and arguments are found in the thesis, positioned near the end of the introduction. Later supporting paragraphs offer relevant quotations, paraphrases, and summaries from primary or secondary sources, which are then interpreted, analyzed, and evaluated. The goal of persuasive writers is not to stack quotes, but to develop original ideas by using sources as a starting point. Good persuasive writing makes powerful arguments with valid sources and thoughtful analysis. Poor persuasive writing is riddled with bias and logical fallacies. Sometimes, logical and illogical arguments are sandwiched together in the same piece. Therefore, readers should display skepticism when reading persuasive arguments.

<u>Genre</u>
Classifying literature involves an understanding of the concept of genre. A *genre* is a category of literature that possesses similarities in style and in characteristics. Based on form and structure, there are four basic genres.

Fictional Prose
Fictional prose consists of fictional works written in standard form with a natural flow of speech and without poetic structure. **Fictional prose** primarily utilizes grammatically complete sentences and a paragraph structure to convey its message.

Drama
Drama is fiction that is written to be performed in a variety of media, intended to be performed for an audience, and structured for that purpose. **Drama** might be composed using poetry or prose, often straddling the elements of both in what actors are expected to present. Action and dialogue are the tools used in drama to tell the story.

Poetry
Poetry is fiction in verse that has a unique focus on the rhythm of language and focuses on intensity of feeling. It is not an entire story, though it may tell one; it is compact in form and in function. **Poetry** can be considered as a poet's brief word picture for a reader. Poetic structure is primarily composed of lines and stanzas. Together, poetic structure and devices are the methods that poets use to lead readers to feeling an effect and, ultimately, to the interpretive message.

Literary Nonfiction
Literary nonfiction is prose writing that is based on current or past real events or real people and includes straightforward accounts as well as those that offer opinions on facts or factual events. The Praxis exam distinguishes between **literary nonfiction**—a form of writing that incorporates literary styles and techniques to create factually-based narratives—and informational texts, which will be addressed in the next section.

Use of Language

<u>Precision</u>
People often think of precision in terms of math, but precise word choice is another key to successful writing. Since language itself is imprecise, it's important for the writer to find the exact word or words to convey the full, intended meaning of a given situation. For example:

> The number of deaths has gone down since seat belt laws started.

There are several problems with this sentence. First, the word *deaths* is too general. From the context, it's assumed that the writer is referring only to deaths caused by car accidents. However, without clarification, the sentence lacks impact and is probably untrue. The phrase "gone down" might be accurate, but a more precise word could provide more information and greater accuracy. Did the numbers show a slow and steady decrease of highway fatalities or a sudden drop? If the latter is true, the writer is missing a chance to make their point more dramatically. Instead of "gone down" they could substitute *plummeted*, *fallen drastically*, or *rapidly diminished* to bring the information to life. Also, the phrase "seat belt laws" is unclear. Does it refer to laws requiring cars to include seat belts or to laws requiring drivers and passengers to use them? Finally, *started* is not a strong verb. Words like *enacted* or *adopted* are more direct and make the content more real.

When put together, these changes create a far more powerful sentence:

> The number of highway fatalities has plummeted since laws requiring seat belt usage were enacted.

However, it's important to note that precise word choice can sometimes be taken too far. If the writer of the sentence above takes precision to an extreme, it might result in the following:

The incidence of high-speed, automobile accident related fatalities has decreased 75% and continued to remain at historical lows since the initial set of federal legislations requiring seat belt use were enacted in 1992.

This sentence is extremely precise, but it takes so long to achieve that precision that it suffers from a lack of clarity. Precise writing is about finding the right balance between information and flow. This is also an issue of conciseness (discussed in the next section).

The last thing to consider with precision is a word choice that's not only unclear or uninteresting, but also confusing or misleading. For example:

The number of highway fatalities has become hugely lower since laws requiring seat belt use were enacted.

In this case, the reader might be confused by the word *hugely*. Huge means large, but here the writer uses *hugely* to describe something small. Though most readers can decipher this, doing so disconnects them from the flow of the writing and makes the writer's point less effective.

Conciseness
"Less is more" is a good rule to follow when writing a sentence. Unfortunately, writers often include extra words and phrases that seem necessary at the time, but add nothing to the main idea. This confuses the reader and creates unnecessary repetition. Writing that lacks conciseness is usually guilty of excessive wordiness and redundant phrases. Here's an example containing both of these issues:

> When legislators decided to begin creating legislation making it mandatory for automobile drivers and passengers to make use of seat belts while in cars, a large number of them made those laws for reasons that were political reasons.

There are several empty or "fluff" words here that take up too much space. These can be eliminated while still maintaining the writer's meaning. For example:

- "Decided to begin" could be shortened to "began"
- "Making it mandatory for" could be shortened to "requiring"
- "Make use of" could be shortened to "use"
- "A large number" could be shortened to "many"

In addition, there are several examples of redundancy that can be eliminated:

- "Legislators decided to begin creating legislation" and "made those laws"
- "Automobile drivers and passengers" and "while in cars"
- "Reasons that were political reasons"

These changes are incorporated as follows:

> When legislators began requiring drivers and passengers to use seat belts, many of them did so for political reasons.

There are many general examples of redundant phrases, such as "add an additional," "complete and total," "time schedule," and "transportation vehicle." If asked to identify a redundant phrase on the test, look for words that are close together with the same (or similar) meanings.

<u>Word Choice</u>
An author's choice of words—also referred to as **diction**—helps to convey his or her meaning in a particular way. Through diction, an author can convey a particular tone—e.g., a humorous tone, a serious tone—in order to support the thesis in a meaningful way to the reader.

Connotation and Denotation
Connotation is when an author chooses words or phrases that invoke ideas or feelings other than their literal meaning. An example of the use of connotation is the word *cheap*, which suggests something is poor in value or negatively describes a person as reluctant to spend money. When something or someone is described this way, the reader is more inclined to have a particular image or feeling about it or him/her. Thus, connotation can be a very effective language tool in creating emotion and swaying opinion. However, connotations are sometimes hard to pin down because varying emotions can be associated with a word. Generally, though, connotative meanings tend to be fairly consistent within a specific cultural group.

Denotation refers to words or phrases that mean exactly what they say. It is helpful when a writer wants to present hard facts or vocabulary terms with which readers may be unfamiliar. Some examples of denotation are the words *inexpensive* and *frugal*. *Inexpensive* refers to the cost of something, not its value, and *frugal* indicates that a person is conscientiously watching his or her spending. These terms do not elicit the same emotions that *cheap* does.

Authors sometimes choose to use both, but what they choose and when they use it is what critical readers need to differentiate. One method isn't inherently better than the other; however, one may create a better effect, depending upon an author's intent. If, for example, an author's purpose is to inform, to instruct, and to familiarize readers with a difficult subject, his or her use of connotation may be helpful. However, it may also undermine credibility and confuse readers. An author who wants to create a credible, scholarly effect in his or her text would most likely use denotation, which emphasizes literal, factual meaning and examples.

Figures of Speech
Another form of non-literal expression can be found in **figures of speech**. As with connotative language, figures of speech tend to be shared within a cultural group and may be difficult to pick up on for learners outside of that group. In some cases, a figure of speech may be based on the literal denotation of the

words it contains, but in other cases, a figure of speech is far removed from its literal meaning. A case in point is **irony**, where what is said is the exact opposite of what is meant:

> The new tax plan is poorly planned, based on faulty economic data, and unable to address the financial struggles of middle class families. Yet legislators remain committed to passing this brilliant proposal.

When the writer refers to the proposal as brilliant, the opposite is implied—the plan is "faulty" and "poorly planned." By using irony, the writer means that the proposal is anything but brilliant by using the word in a non-literal sense.

Another figure of speech is **hyperbole**—extreme exaggeration or overstatement. Statements like, "I love you to the moon and back" or "Let's be friends for a million years" utilize hyperbole to convey a greater depth of emotion, without literally committing oneself to space travel or a life of immortality.

Figures of speech may sometimes use one word in place of another. **Synecdoche**, for example, uses a part of something to refer to its whole. The expression "Don't hurt a hair on her head!" implies protecting more than just an individual hair, but rather her entire body. "The art teacher is training a class of Picassos" uses Picasso, one individual notable artist, to stand in for the entire category of talented artists. Another figure of speech using word replacement is **metonymy**, where a word is replaced with something closely associated to it. For example, news reports may use the word "Washington" to refer to the American government or "the crown" to refer to the British monarch.

Technical Language
Test takers and critical readers alike should be very aware of technical language used within informational text. **Technical language** refers to terminology that is specific to a particular industry and is best understood by those specializing in that industry. This language is fairly easy to differentiate, since it will most likely be unfamiliar to readers. It's critical to be able to define technical language either by the author's written definition, through the use of an included glossary—if offered—or through context clues that help readers clarify word meaning.

Words in Context

There will be many occasions in one's reading career in which an unknown word or a word with multiple meanings will pop up. There are ways of determining what these words or phrases mean that do not require the use of the dictionary, which is especially helpful during a test where one may not be available. Even outside of the exam, knowing how to derive an understanding of a word via context clues will be a critical skill in the real world. The context is the circumstances in which a story or a passage is happening, and can usually be found in the series of words directly before or directly after the word or phrase in question. The clues are the words that hint towards the meaning of the unknown word or phrase.

There may be questions that ask about the meaning of a particular word or phrase within a passage. There are a couple ways to approach these kinds of questions:

1. Define the word or phrase in a way that is easy to comprehend (using context clues).
2. Try out each answer choice in place of the word.

To demonstrate, here's an example from *Alice in Wonderland*:

> Alice was beginning to get very tired of sitting by her sister on the bank, and of having nothing to do: once or twice she <u>peeped</u> into the book her sister was reading, but it had no pictures or conversations in it, "and what is the use of a book," thought Alice, "without pictures or conversations?"

Q: As it is used in the selection, the word <u>peeped</u> means:

Using the first technique, before looking at the answers, define the word "peeped" using context clues and then find the matching answer. Then, analyze the entire passage in order to determine the meaning, not just the surrounding words.

To begin, imagine a blank where the word should be and put a synonym or definition there: "once or twice she _____ into the book her sister was reading." The context clue here is the book. It may be tempting to put "read" where the blank is, but notice the preposition word, "into." One does not read *into* a book, one simply reads a book, and since reading a book requires that it is seen with a pair of eyes, then "look" would make the most sense to put into the blank: "once or twice she <u>looked </u>into the book her sister was reading."

Once an easy-to-understand word or synonym has been supplanted, readers should check to make sure it makes sense with the rest of the passage. What happened after she looked into the book? She thought to herself how a book without pictures or conversations is useless. This situation in its entirety makes sense.

Now check the answer choices for a match:
   a. To make a high-pitched cry
   b. To smack
   c. To look curiously
   d. To pout

Since the word was already defined, Choice *C* is the best option.

Using the second technique, replace the figurative blank with each of the answer choices and determine which one is the most appropriate. Remember to look further into the passage to clarify that they work, because they could still make sense out of context.
   a. Once or twice she <u>made a high pitched cry</u> into the book her sister was reading
   b. Once or twice she <u>smacked</u> into the book her sister was reading
   c. Once or twice she <u>looked curiously</u> into the book her sister was reading
   d. Once or twice she <u>pouted</u> into the book her sister was reading

For Choice *A*, it does not make much sense in any context for a person to yell into a book, unless maybe something terrible has happened in the story. Given that afterward Alice thinks to herself how useless a book without pictures is, this option does not make sense within context.

For Choice *B*, smacking a book someone is reading may make sense if the rest of the passage indicates a reason for doing so. If Alice was angry or her sister had shoved it in her face, then maybe smacking the book would make sense within context. However, since whatever she does with the book causes her to think, "what is the use of a book without pictures or conversations?" then answer Choice *B* is not an appropriate answer. Answer Choice *C* fits well within context, given her subsequent thoughts on the matter. Answer Choice *D* does not make sense in context or grammatically, as people do not "pout into" things.

This is a simple example to illustrate the techniques outlined above. There may, however, be a question in which all of the definitions are correct and also make sense out of context, in which the appropriate context clues will really need to be honed in on in order to determine the correct answer. For example, here is another passage from *Alice in Wonderland*:

> . . . but when the Rabbit actually took a watch out of its waistcoat pocket, and looked at it, and then hurried on, Alice <u>started</u> to her feet, for it flashed across her mind that she had never before seen a rabbit with either a waistcoat-pocket or a watch to take out of it, and burning with curiosity, she ran across the field after it, and was just in time to see it pop down a large rabbit-hole under the hedge.

Q: As it is used in the passage, the word started means
   a. To turn on
   b. To begin
   c. To move quickly
   d. To be surprised

All of these words qualify as a definition of "start," but using context clues, the correct answer can be identified using one of the two techniques above. It's easy to see that one does not turn on, begin, or be surprised to one's feet. The selection also states that she "ran across the field after it," indicating that she was in a hurry. Therefore, to move quickly would make the most sense in this context.

The same strategies can be applied to vocabulary that may be completely unfamiliar. In this case, focus on the words before or after the unknown word in order to determine its definition. Take this sentence, for example:

> Sam was such a <u>miser</u> that he forced Andrew to pay him twelve cents for the candy, even though he had a large inheritance and he knew his friend was poor.

Unlike with assertion questions, for vocabulary questions, it may be necessary to apply some critical thinking skills that may not be explicitly stated within the passage. Think about the implications of the passage, or what the text is trying to say. With this example, it is important to realize that it is considered unusually stingy for a person to demand so little money from someone instead of just letting their friend have the candy, especially if this person is already wealthy. Hence, a <u>miser</u> is a greedy or stingy individual.

Questions about complex vocabulary may not be explicitly asked, but this is a useful skill to know. If there is an unfamiliar word while reading a passage and its definition goes unknown, it is possible to miss out on a critical message that could inhibit the ability to appropriately answer the questions. Practicing this technique in daily life will sharpen this ability to derive meanings from context clues with ease.

<u>Affixes</u>

Individual words are constructed from building blocks of meaning. An **affix** is an element that is added to a root or stem word that can change the word's meaning.

For example, the stem word *fix* is a verb meaning *to repair*. When the ending –*able* is added, it becomes the adjective *fixable*, meaning "capable of being repaired." Adding *un*– to the beginning changes the word to *unfixable*, meaning "incapable of being repaired." In this way, affixes attach to the word stem to create a new word and a new meaning. Knowledge of affixes can assist in deciphering the meaning of unfamiliar words.

Affixes are also related to inflection. **Inflection** is the modification of a base word to express a different grammatical or syntactical function. For example, countable nouns such as *car* and *airport* become plural with the addition of –*s* at the end: *cars* and *airports*.

Verb tense is also expressed through inflection. **Regular verbs**—those that follow a standard inflection pattern—can be changed to past tense using the affixes –*ed*, –*d*, or –*ied*, as in *cooked* and *studied*. Verbs can also be modified for continuous tenses by using –*ing*, as in *working* or *exploring*. Thus, affixes are used not only to express meaning but also to reflect a word's grammatical purpose.

A **prefix** is an affix attached to the beginning of a word. The meanings of English prefixes mainly come from Greek and Latin origins. The chart below contains a few of the most commonly used English prefixes.

Prefix	Meaning	Example
a-	Not	amoral, asymptomatic
anti-	Against	antidote, antifreeze
auto-	Self	automobile, automatic
circum-	Around	circumference, circumspect
co-, com-, con-	Together	coworker, companion
contra-	Against	contradict, contrary
de-	negation or reversal	deflate, deodorant
extra-	outside, beyond	extraterrestrial, extracurricular
in-, im-, il-, ir-	Not	impossible, irregular
inter-	Between	international, intervene
intra-	Within	intramural, intranet
mis-	Wrongly	mistake, misunderstand
mono-	One	monolith, monopoly
non-	Not	nonpartisan, nonsense
pre-	Before	preview, prediction
re-	Again	review, renew
semi-	Half	semicircle, semicolon
sub-	Under	subway, submarine
super-	Above	superhuman, superintendent
trans-	across, beyond, through	trans-Siberian, transform
un-	Not	unwelcome, unfriendly

While the addition of a prefix alters the meaning of the base word, the addition of a **suffix** may also affect a word's part of speech. For example, adding a suffix can change the noun *material* into the verb *materialize* and back to a noun again in *materialization*.

Suffix	Part of Speech	Meaning	Example
-able, -ible	adjective	having the ability to	honorable, flexible
-acy, -cy	noun	state or quality	intimacy, dependency
-al, -ical	adjective	having the quality of	historical, tribal
-en	verb	to cause to become	strengthen, embolden
-er, -ier	adjective	comparative	happier, longer
-est, -iest	adjective	superlative	sunniest, hottest
-ess	noun	female	waitress, actress
-ful	adjective	full of, characterized by	beautiful, thankful
-fy, -ify	verb	to cause, to come to be	liquefy, intensify
-ism	noun	doctrine, belief, action	Communism, Buddhism
-ive, -ative, -itive	adjective	having the quality of	creative, innovative
-ize	verb	to convert into, to subject to	Americanize, dramatize
-less	adjective	without, missing	emotionless, hopeless
-ly	adverb	in the manner of	quickly, energetically
-ness	noun	quality or state	goodness, darkness
-ous, -ious, -eous	adjective	having the quality of	spontaneous, pious
-ship	noun	status or condition	partnership, ownership
-tion	noun	action or state	renovation, promotion
-y	adjective	characterized by	smoky, dreamy

Through knowledge of prefixes and suffixes, a student's vocabulary can be instantly expanded with an understanding of **etymology**—the origin of words. This, in turn, can be used to add sentence structure variety to academic writing.

Narrative Point of View

Point of view is an important writing device to consider. In fiction writing, point of view refers to who tells the story or from whose perspective readers are observing as they read. In non-fiction writing, the **point of view** refers to whether the author refers to himself/herself, his/her readers, or chooses not to refer to either. Whether fiction or nonfiction, the author will carefully consider the impact the perspective will have on the purpose and main point of the writing.

- *First-person point of view*: The story is told from the narrator's perspective. In fiction, this would mean that the main character is also the narrator. First-person point of view is easily recognized by the use of personal pronouns such as *I, me, we, us, our, my*, and *myself*.

- *Third-person point of view*: In a more formal essay, this would be an appropriate perspective because the focus should be on the subject matter, not the writer or the reader. Third-person point of view is recognized by the use of the pronouns *he, she, they,* and *it*. In fiction writing, third person point of view has a few variations.

- *Third-person limited* point of view refers to a story told by a narrator who has access to the thoughts and feelings of just one character.

- In *third-person omniscient* point of view, the narrator has access to the thoughts and feelings of all the characters.

- In *third-person objective* point of view, the narrator is like a fly on the wall and can see and hear what the characters do and say but does not have access to their thoughts and feelings.

- *Second-person point of view* isn't commonly used in fiction or non-fiction writing because it directly addresses the reader using the pronouns *you, your,* and *yourself*. Second-person perspective is more appropriate in direct communication, such as business letters or emails.

Point of View	Pronouns Used
First person	I, me, we, us, our, my, myself
Second person	You, your, yourself
Third person	He, she, it, they

Tone
Tone refers to the writer's attitude toward the subject matter. **Tone** is usually explained in terms of a work of fiction. For example, the tone conveys how the writer feels about their characters and the situations in which they're involved. Nonfiction writing is sometimes thought to have no tone at all; however, this is incorrect.

A lot of nonfiction writing has a neutral tone, which is an important tone for the writer to take. A neutral tone demonstrates that the writer is presenting a topic impartially and letting the information speak for itself. On the other hand, nonfiction writing can be just as effective and appropriate if the tone isn't neutral. For instance, take this example involving seat belts:

> Seat belts save more lives than any other automobile safety feature. Many studies show that airbags save lives as well; however, not all cars have airbags. For instance, some older cars don't. Furthermore, air bags aren't entirely reliable. For example, studies show that in 15% of accidents airbags don't deploy as designed, but, on the other hand, seat belt malfunctions are extremely rare. The number of highway fatalities has plummeted since laws requiring seat belt usage were enacted.

In this passage, the writer mostly chooses to retain a neutral tone when presenting information. If the writer would instead include their own personal experience of losing a friend or family member in a car accident, the tone would change dramatically. The tone would no longer be neutral and would show that the writer has a personal stake in the content, allowing them to interpret the information in a different way. When analyzing tone, consider what the writer is trying to achieve in the text and how they create the tone using style.

Characterization

Authors use characterization in literature to develop the traits of the characters. **Characterization** refers to the way a character's personality is revealed and developed. The development of these traits is what makes a character seem real to readers. Characters can be revealed either directly or indirectly. **Direct**, or explicit, characterization is when an author reveals a character's traits up front through description by the narrator or another character. **Indirect**, or implicit, characterization can be revealed more subtly through a character's actions, words, or appearance or interactions with other characters. Readers need to infer the characterization when it is revealed indirectly. Certain characters may be more fully developed than others. For example, the main character is likely very well developed, whereas a minor secondary character may have much more limited characterization. Readers may know many details about the personality of the main character, while they would only be given a brief description of a character who matters less to the plot. Different genres of literature also have varying levels of character development. For example, a poet may use very limited characterization, while a playwright may include long detailed descriptions of each character as relevant to the production of the play.

In poetry, characterization is the way a poet introduces the personality of the main character or secondary characters in the poem. Poems typically only have one character, but longer poems, such as an epic, can have one or more secondary characters. The main character in a poem using first person point of view is called the **speaker** or persona. He or she is not to be confused with the poet, as they are two separate entities. Characterization can be revealed directly or indirectly. Direct characterization involves the poet explicitly stating the character's traits. Indirect characterization is revealed only through the character's words or actions in the poem. Unlike drama or prose, poetry is often brief and does not allow for long descriptions of characters. Character traits are revealed through very brief descriptions, even just a line or two, or through literary devices such as rhyme, or the imagery used in the poem.

Critical Analysis

Main Ideas and Supporting Details

Topics and main ideas are critical parts of writing. The **topic** is the subject matter of the piece. An example of a topic would be *the use of cell phones in a classroom*.

The **main idea** is what the writer wants to say about that topic. A writer may make the point that the use of cell phones in a classroom is a serious problem that must be addressed in order for students to learn better. Therefore, the topic is cell phone usage in a classroom, and the main idea is that it's *a serious problem needing to be addressed*. The topic can be expressed in a word or two, but the main idea should be a complete thought.

An author will likely identify the topic immediately within the title or the first sentence of the passage. The main idea is usually presented in the introduction. In a single passage, the main idea may be identified in the first or last sentence, but it will most likely be directly stated and easily recognized by the reader. Because it is not always stated immediately in a passage, it's important that readers carefully read the entire passage to identify the main idea.

The main idea should not be confused with the thesis statement. A **thesis statement** is a clear statement of the writer's specific stance and can often be found in the introduction of a nonfiction piece. The thesis is a specific sentence (or two) that offers the direction and focus of the discussion.

In order to illustrate the main idea, a writer will use **supporting details**, which provide evidence or examples to help make a point. Supporting details are typically found in nonfiction pieces that seek to inform or persuade the reader.

In the example of cell phone usage in the classroom, where the author's main idea is to show the seriousness of this problem and the need to "unplug", supporting details would be critical for effectively making that point. Supporting details used here might include statistics on a decline in student focus and studies showing the impact of digital technology usage on students' attention spans. The author could also include testimonies from teachers surveyed on the topic.

It's important that readers evaluate the author's supporting details to be sure that they are credible, provide evidence of the author's point, and directly support the main idea. Although shocking statistics grab readers' attention, their use may provide ineffective information in the piece. Details like this are crucial to understanding the passage and evaluating how well the author presents his or her argument and evidence.

Also remember that when most authors write, they want to make a point or send a message. This point or message of a text is known as the theme. Authors may state themes explicitly, like in *Aesop's Fables*. More often, especially in modern literature, readers must infer the theme based on text details. Usually after carefully reading and analyzing an entire text, the theme emerges. Typically, the longer the piece, the more themes you will encounter, though often one theme dominates the rest, as evidenced by the author's purposeful revisiting of it throughout the passage.

Text Evidence

Text evidence is the information readers find in a text or passage that supports the main idea or point(s) in a story. In turn, text evidence can help readers draw conclusions about the text or passage. The information should be taken directly from the text or passage and placed in quotation marks. Text evidence provides readers with information to support ideas about the text so that they do not rely simply on their own thoughts. Details should be precise, descriptive, and factual. Statistics are a great piece of text evidence because they provide readers with exact numbers and not just a generalization. For example, instead of saying "Asia has a larger population than Europe," authors could provide detailed information such as, "In Asia there are over 4 billion people, whereas in Europe there are a little over 750 million." More definitive information provides better evidence to readers to help support their conclusions about texts or passages.

Text Credibility

Credible sources are important when drawing conclusions because readers need to be able to trust what they are reading. Authors should always use credible sources to help gain the trust of their readers. A text is **credible** when it is believable and the author is objective and unbiased. If readers do not trust an author's words, they may simply dismiss the text completely. For example, if an author writes a persuasive essay, he or she is outwardly trying to sway readers' opinions to align with his or her own. Readers may agree or disagree with the author, which may, in turn, lead them to believe that the author is credible or not credible. Also, readers should keep in mind the source of the text. If readers review a journal about astronomy, would a more reliable source be a NASA employee or a medical doctor? Overall, text credibility is important when drawing conclusions, because readers want reliable sources that support the decisions they have made about the author's ideas.

Author's Intent

No matter the genre or format, all authors are writing to persuade, inform, entertain, or express feelings. Often, these purposes are blended, with one dominating the rest. It's useful to learn to recognize the author's intent.

Persuasive writing is used to persuade or convince readers of something. It often contains two elements: the argument and the counterargument. The argument takes a stance on an issue, while the counterargument pokes holes in the opposition's stance. Authors rely on logic, emotion, and writer credibility to persuade readers to agree with them. If readers are opposed to the stance before reading, they are unlikely to adopt that stance. However, those who are undecided or committed to the same stance are more likely to agree with the author.

Informative writing tries to teach or inform. Workplace manuals, instructor lessons, statistical reports and cookbooks are examples of informative texts. Informative writing is usually based on facts and is often void of emotion and persuasion. Informative texts generally contain statistics, charts, and graphs. Though most informative texts lack a persuasive agenda, readers must examine the text carefully to determine whether one exists within a given passage.

Stories or narratives are designed to entertain. When you go to the movies, you often want to escape for a few hours, not necessarily to think critically. Entertaining writing is designed to delight and engage the reader. However, sometimes this type of writing can be woven into more serious materials, such as persuasive or informative writing to hook the reader before transitioning into a more scholarly discussion.

Emotional writing works to evoke the reader's feelings, such as anger, euphoria, or sadness. The connection between reader and author is an attempt to cause the reader to share the author's intended emotion or tone. Sometimes in order to make a piece more poignant, the author simply wants readers to feel emotion that the author has felt. Other times, the author attempts to persuade or manipulate the reader into adopting his stance. While it's okay to sympathize with the author, be aware of the individual's underlying intent.

Identifying Modes of Writing

<u>Distinguishing Between Common Modes of Writing</u>
To distinguish between the common modes of writing, it is important to identify the primary purpose of the work. This can be determined by considering what the author is trying to say to the reader. Although there are countless different styles of writing, all written works tend to fall under four primary categories: argumentative/persuasive, informative expository, descriptive, and narrative.

The table below highlights the purpose, distinct characteristics, and examples of each rhetorical mode.

Writing Mode	Purpose	Distinct Characteristics	Examples
Argumentative	To persuade	Opinions, loaded or subjective language, evidence, suggestions of what the reader should do, calls to action	Critical reviews Political journals Letters of recommendation Cover letters Advertising
Informative	To teach or inform	Objective language, definitions, instructions, factual information	Business and scientific reports Textbooks Instruction manuals News articles Personal letters Wills Informative essays Travel guides Study guides
Descriptive	To deliver sensory details to the reader	Heavy use of adjectives and imagery, language that appeals to any of the five senses	Poetry Journal entries Often used in narrative mode
Narrative	To tell a story, share an experience, entertain	Series of events, plot, characters, dialogue, conflict	Novels Short stories Novellas Anecdotes Biographies Epic poems Autobiographies

Identifying Common Types of Writing

The following steps help to identify examples of common types within the modes of writing:

1. Identifying the audience—to whom or for whom the author is writing
2. Determining the author's purpose—why the author is writing the piece
3. Analyzing the word choices and how they are used

To demonstrate, the following passage has been marked to illustrate *the addressee*, the author's purpose, and word choices:

To Whom It May Concern:

I am extraordinarily excited to be applying to the Master of Environmental Science program at Australian National University. I believe the richness in biological and cultural diversity, as well as Australia's close proximity to the Great Barrier Reef, would provide a deeply fulfilling educational experience. *I am writing to express why I believe I would be an <u>excellent</u> addition to the program.*

While in college, I participated in a three-month public health internship in Ecuador, where I spent time both learning about medicine in a third world country and also about the Ecuadorian environment, including the Amazon Jungle and the Galápagos Islands. <u>My favorite experience</u> through the internship, besides swimming with sea lions in San Cristóbal, was helping to neutralize parasitic potable water and collect samples for analysis in Puyo.

Though my undergraduate studies related primarily to the human body, I took several courses in natural science, including a year of chemistry, biology, and physics as well as a course in a calculus. <u>I am confident</u> that my fundamental knowledge in these fields will prepare me for the science courses integral to the Masters of Environmental Science.

Having identified the *addressee*, it is evident that this selection is a letter of some kind. Further inspection into the author's purpose, seen in *italics*, shows that the author is trying to explain why he or she should be accepted into the environmental science program, which automatically places it into the argumentative mode as the writer is trying to persuade the reader to agree and to incite the reader into action by encouraging the program to accept the writer as a candidate. In addition to revealing the purpose, the use of emotional language—extraordinarily, excellent, deeply fulfilling, favorite experience, confident—illustrates that this is a persuasive piece. It also provides evidence for why this person would be an excellent addition to the program—his/her experience in Ecuador and with scientific curriculum.

The following passage presents an opportunity to solidify this method of analysis and practice the steps above to determine the mode of writing:

The biological effects of laughter have long been an interest of medicine and psychology. Laughing is often speculated to reduce blood pressure because it induces feelings of relaxation and elation. Participating students watched a series of videos that elicited laughter, and their blood pressure was taken before and after the viewings. An average decrease in blood pressure was observed, though resulting p-values attest that the results were not significant.

This selection contains factual and scientific information, is devoid of any adjectives or flowery descriptions, and is not trying to convince the reader of any particular stance. Though the audience is not directly addressed, the purpose of the passage is to present the results of an experiment to those who would be interested in the biological effects of laughter—most likely a scientific community. Thus, this passage is an example of informative writing.

Below is another passage to help identify examples of the common writing modes, taken from *The Endeavor Journal of Sir Joseph Banks*:

10th May 1769 – THE ENGLISH CREW GET TAHITIAN NAMES

We have now got the Indian name of the Island, Otahite, so therefore for the future I shall call it. As for our own names the Indians find so much dificulty in pronouncing them that we are forcd to indulge them in calling us what they please, or rather what they say when they attempt to pronounce them. I give here the List: Captn Cooke *Toote*, Dr Solander *Torano*, Mr Hicks *Hete*, Mr Gore *Toárro*, Mr Molineux *Boba* from his Christian name Robert, Mr Monkhouse *Mato*, and myself *Tapáne*. In this manner they have names for almost every man in the ship.

This extract contains no elements of an informative or persuasive intent and does not seem to follow any particular line of narrative. The passage gives a list of the different names that the Indians have given the crew members, as well as the name of an island. Although there is no context for the selection, through the descriptions, it is clear that the author and his comrades are on an island trying to communicate with the native inhabitants. Hence, this passage is a journal that reflects the descriptive mode.

These are only a few of the many examples that can be found in the four primary modes of writing.

Determining the Appropriate Mode of Writing

The author's **primary purpose** is defined as the reason an author chooses to write a selection, and it is often dependent on his or her **audience**. A biologist writing a textbook, for example, does so to communicate scientific knowledge to an audience of people who want to study biology. An audience can be as broad as the entire global population or as specific as women fighting for equal rights in the bicycle repair industry. Whatever the audience, it is important that the author considers its demographics—age, gender, culture, language, education level, etc.

If the author's purpose is to persuade or inform, he or she will consider how much the intended audience knows about the subject. For example, if an author is writing on the importance of recycling to anyone who will listen, he or she will use the informative mode—including background information on recycling—and the argumentative mode—evidence for why it works, while also using simple diction so that it is easy for everyone to understand. If, on the other hand, the writer is proposing new methods for recycling using solar energy, the audience is probably already familiar with standard recycling processes and will require less background information, as well as more technical language inherent to the scientific community.

If the author's purpose is to entertain through a story or a poem, he or she will need to consider whom he/she is trying to entertain. If an author is writing a script for a children's cartoon, the plot, language, conflict, characters, and humor would align with the interests of the age demographic of that audience. On the other hand, if an author is trying to entertain adults, he or she may write content not suitable for children. The author's purpose and audience are generally interdependent.

Inferences in a Text

Readers should be able to make **inferences**. Making an inference requires the reader to read between the lines and look for what is *implied* rather than what is directly stated. That is, using information that is known from the text, the reader is able to make a logical assumption about information that is *not* directly stated but is probably true. Read the following passage:

"Hey, do you wanna meet my new puppy?" Jonathan asked.

"Oh, I'm sorry but please don't—" Jacinta began to protest, but before she could finish, Jonathan had already opened the passenger side door of his car and a perfect white ball of fur came bouncing towards Jacinta.

"Isn't he the cutest?" beamed Jonathan.

"Yes—achoo!—he's pretty—aaaachooo!!—adora—aaa—aaaachoo!" Jacinta managed to say in between sneezes. "But if you don't mind, I—I—achoo!—need to go inside."

Which of the following can be inferred from Jacinta's reaction to the puppy?
- a. she hates animals
- b. she is allergic to dogs
- c. she prefers cats to dogs
- d. she is angry at Jonathan

An inference requires the reader to consider the information presented and then form their own idea about what is probably true. Based on the details in the passage, what is the best answer to the question? Important details to pay attention to include the tone of Jacinta's dialogue, which is overall polite and apologetic, as well as her reaction itself, which is a long string of sneezes. Answer choices (a) and (d) both express strong emotions ("hates" and "angry") that are not evident in Jacinta's speech or actions. Answer choice (c) mentions cats, but there is nothing in the passage to indicate Jacinta's feelings about cats. Answer choice (b), "she is allergic to dogs," is the most logical choice—based on the fact that she began sneezing as soon as a fluffy dog approached her, it makes sense to guess that Jacinta might be allergic to dogs. So even though Jacinta never directly states, "Sorry, I'm allergic to dogs!" using the clues in the passage, it is still reasonable to guess that this is true.

Making inferences is crucial for readers of literature, because literary texts often avoid presenting complete and direct information to readers about characters' thoughts or feelings, or they present this information in an unclear way, leaving it up to the reader to interpret clues given in the text. In order to make inferences while reading, readers should ask themselves:

- What details are being presented in the text?
- Is there any important information that seems to be missing?
- Based on the information that the author *does* include, what else is probably true?
- Is this inference reasonable based on what is already known?

Apply Information

A natural extension of being able to make an inference from a given set of information is also being able to apply that information to a new context. This is especially useful in non-fiction or informative writing. Considering the facts and details presented in the text, readers should consider how the same information might be relevant in a different situation. The following is an example of applying an inferential conclusion to a different context:

> Often, individuals behave differently in large groups than they do as individuals. One example of this is the psychological phenomenon known as the bystander effect. According to the bystander effect, the more people who witness an accident or crime occur, the less likely each individual bystander is to respond or offer assistance to the victim. A classic example of this is the murder of Kitty Genovese in New York City in the 1960s. Although there were over thirty witnesses to her killing by a stabber, none of them intervened to help Kitty or contact the police.

Considering the phenomenon of the bystander effect, what would probably happen if somebody tripped on the stairs in a crowded subway station?
- a. Everybody would stop to help the person who tripped
- b. Bystanders would point and laugh at the person who tripped
- c. Someone would call the police after walking away from the station
- d. Few if any bystanders would offer assistance to the person who tripped

This question asks readers to apply the information they learned from the passage, which is an informative paragraph about the bystander effect. According to the passage, this is a concept in psychology that describes the way people in groups respond to an accident—the more people are present, the less likely any one person is to intervene. While the passage illustrates this effect with the example of a woman's murder, the question asks readers to apply it to a different context—in this case, someone falling down the stairs in front of many subway passengers. Although this specific situation is not discussed in the passage, readers should be able to apply the general concepts described in the paragraph. The definition of the bystander effect includes any instance of an accident or crime in front of a large group of people. The question asks about a situation that falls within the same definition, so the general concept should still hold true: in the midst of a large crowd, few individuals are likely to actually respond to an accident. In this case, answer choice (d) is the best response.

Prose

Fiction

Elements of Fiction

<u>Literary Elements of Fiction</u>
There is no one, final definition of what literary elements are. They can be considered features or characteristics of fiction, but they are really more of a way that readers can unpack a text for the purpose of analysis and understanding the meaning. The elements contribute to a reader's literary interpretation of a passage as to how they function to convey the central message of a work. The most common literary elements used for analysis are the following:

- The **theme** is the central message of a fictional work, whether that work is structured as prose, drama, or poetry. It is the heart of what an author is trying to say to readers through the writing, and theme is largely conveyed through literary elements and techniques. Poetic elements overlap these elements and will be addressed separately.

- The **plot** is what happens in the story. Plots may be singular, containing one problem, or they may be very complex, with many sub-plots. All plots have exposition, a conflict, a climax, and a resolution. The *conflict* drives the plot and is something that the reader expects to be resolved. The plot carries those events along until there is a resolution to the conflict.

- **Characters** are the story's figures that assume primary, secondary, or minor roles. **Central** or major characters are those integral to the story—the plot cannot be resolved without them. A central character can be a **protagonist** or hero. There may be more than one protagonist, and he/she doesn't always have to possess good characteristics. A character can also be an **antagonist**—the force against a protagonist.

  Dynamic characters change over the course of the plot time. *Static* characters do not change. A **symbolic** character is one that represents an author's idea about society in general—e.g., Napoleon in Orwell's *Animal Farm*. **Stock** characters are those that appear across genres and embrace stereotypes—e.g., the cowboy of the Wild West or the blonde bombshell in a detective novel. A **flat** character is one that does not present a lot of complexity or depth, while a **rounded** character does. Sometimes, the **narrator** of a story or the speaker in a poem can be a character—e.g., Nick Carraway in Fitzgerald's *The Great Gatsby* or the speaker in Browning's "My Last Duchess." The narrator might also function as a character in prose, though not be part of the story—e.g., Dicken's narrator of *A Christmas Carol*.

- The **setting** is the time, place, or set of surroundings in which the story occurs. It includes time or time span, place(s), climates, geography—man-made or natural—or cultural environments. Emily Dickenson's poem "Because I could not stop for Death" has a simple setting—the narrator's symbolic ride with Death through town towards the local graveyard. Conversely, Leo Tolstoy's War and Peace encompasses numerous settings within settings in the areas affected by the Napoleonic Wars, spanning 1805 to 1812.

- The **point of view** is the position the narrator takes when telling the story in prose. If a narrator is incorporated in a drama, the point of view may vary; in poetry, point of view refers to the position the speaker in a poem takes.

  - The **first person** point of view is when the writer uses the word "I" in the text. Poetry often uses first person, e.g., William Wordsworth's "I Wandered Lonely as a Cloud." Two examples of prose written in first person are Suzanne Collins' *The Hunger Games* and Anthony Burgess's *A Clockwork Orange*.

  - The **second person** point of view is when the writer uses the pronoun "you." It is not widely used in prose fiction, but as a technique, it has been used by writers such as William Faulkner in *Absalom, Absalom* and Albert Camus in *The Fall*. It is more common in poetry—e.g., Pablo Neruda's "If You Forget Me."

  - **Third person** point of view is when the writer utilizes pronouns such as him, her, or them. It may be the most utilized point of view in prose as it provides flexibility to an author and is the one with which readers are most familiar. There are two main types of third person used in fiction:

    - *Third person omniscient*—narrator is all-knowing, relating the story by conveying and interpreting thoughts/feelings of all characters

    - *Third person limited*—narrator relates the story through the perspective of one character's thoughts/feelings, usually the main character

Fictional Prose

Fictional Prose
Fiction written in prose can be further broken down into **fiction genres**—types of fiction. Some of the more common genres of fiction are as follows:

- **Classical fiction**: a work of fiction considered timeless in its message or theme, remaining noteworthy and meaningful over decades or centuries—e.g., Charlotte Brontë's *Jane Eyre*, Mark Twain's *Adventures of Huckleberry Finn*

- **Fables**: short fiction that generally features animals, fantastic creatures, or other forces within nature that assume human-like characters and has a moral lesson for the reader—e.g., *Aesop's Fables*

- **Fairy tales**: children's stories with magical characters in imaginary, enchanted lands, usually depicting a struggle between good and evil, a sub-genre of folklore—e.g., Hans Christian Anderson's *The Little Mermaid*, *Cinderella* by the Brothers Grimm

- **Fantasy**: fiction with magic or supernatural elements that cannot occur in the real world, sometimes involving medieval elements in language, usually includes some form of sorcery or witchcraft and sometimes set on a different world—e.g., J.R.R. Tolkien's *The Hobbit*, J.K. Rowling's *Harry Potter and the Sorcerer's Stone*, George R.R. Martin's *A Game of Thrones*

- **Folklore**: types of fiction passed down from oral tradition, stories indigenous to a particular region or culture, with a local flavor in tone, designed to help humans cope with their condition in life and validate cultural traditions, beliefs, and customs—e.g., William Laughead's *Paul Bunyan and The Blue Ox*, the Buddhist story of "The Banyan Deer"

- **Mythology**: closely related to folklore but more widespread, features mystical, otherworldly characters and addresses the basic question of why and how humans exist, relies heavily on allegory and features gods or heroes captured in some sort of struggle—e.g., Greek myths, Genesis I and II in the Bible, Arthurian legends

- **Science fiction**: fiction that uses the principle of extrapolation—loosely defined as a form of prediction—to imagine future realities and problems of the human experience—e.g., Robert Heinlein's *Stranger in a Strange Land*, Ayn Rand's *Anthem*, Isaac Asimov's *I, Robot*, Philip K. Dick's *Do Androids Dream of Electric Sheep?*

- **Short stories**: short works of prose fiction with fully-developed themes and characters, focused on mood, generally developed with a single plot, with a short period of time for settings—e.g., Edgar Allan Poe's "Fall of the House of Usher," Shirley Jackson's "The Lottery," Isaac Bashevis Singer's "Gimpel the Fool"

Identifying Literary Contexts

Understanding that works of literature emerged either because of a particular context—or perhaps despite a context—is key to analyzing them effectively.

Historical Context
The **historical context** of a piece of literature can refer to the time period, setting, or conditions of living at the time it was written as well as the context of the work. For example, Hawthorne's *The Scarlet Letter* was published in 1850, though the setting of the story is 1642-1649. Historically, then, when Hawthorne wrote his novel, the United States found itself at odds as the beginnings of a potential Civil War were in view. Thus, the historical context is potentially significant as it pertains to the ideas of traditions and values, which Hawthorne addresses in his story of Hester Prynne in the era of Puritanism.

Cultural Context
The **cultural context** of a piece of literature refers to cultural factors, such as the beliefs, religions, and customs that surround and are in a work of literature. The Puritan's beliefs, religion, and customs in Hawthorne's novel would be significant as they are at the core of the plot—the reason Hester wears the A and why Arthur kills himself. The customs of people in the Antebellum Period, though not quite as restrictive, were still somewhat similar. This would impact how the audience of the time received the novel.

Literary Context
Literary context refers to the consideration of the genre, potentially at the time the work was written. In 1850, Realism and Romanticism were the driving forces in literature in the U.S., with depictions of life as it was at the time in which the work was written or the time it was written *about* as well as some works celebrating the beauty of nature. Thus, an audience in Hawthorne's time would have been well satisfied with the elements of both offered in the text. They would have been looking for details about everyday things and people (Realism), but they also would appreciate his approach to description of nature and the focus on the individual (American Romanticism). The contexts would be significant as they would pertain to evaluating the work against those criteria.

Here are some questions to use when considering context:

- When was the text written?
- What was society like at the time the text was written, or what was it like, given the work's identified time period?
- Who or what influenced the writer?
- What political or social influences might there have been?
- What influences may there have been in the genre that may have affected the writer?

Additionally, test takers should familiarize themselves with literary periods such as Old and Middle English, American Colonial, American Renaissance, American Naturalistic, and British and American Modernist and Post-Modernist movements. Most students of literature will have had extensive exposure to these literary periods in history, and while it is not necessary to recognize every major literary work on sight and associate that work to its corresponding movement or cultural context, the test taker should be familiar enough with the historical and cultural significance of each test passage in order to be able to address test questions correctly.

The following brief description of some literary contexts and their associated literary examples follows. It is not an all-inclusive list. The test taker should read each description, then follow up with independent study to clarify each movement, its context, its most familiar authors, and their works.

Metaphysical Poetry

Metaphysical poetry is the descriptor applied to 17th century poets whose poetry emphasized the lyrical quality of their work. These works contain highly creative poetic conceits or metaphoric comparisons between two highly dissimilar things or ideas. **Metaphysical poetry** is characterized by highly prosaic language and complicated, often layered, metaphor.

Poems such as John Donne's "The Flea," Andrew Marvell's "To His Coy Mistress," George Herbert's "The Collar," Henry Vaughan's "The World," and Richard Crashaw's "A Song" are associated with this type of poetry.

British Romanticism

British Romanticism was a cultural and literary movement within Europe that developed at the end of the 18th century and extended into the 19th century. It occurred partly in response to aristocratic, political, and social norms and partly in response to the Industrial Revolution of the day. Characterized by intense emotion, major literary works of **British Romanticism** embrace the idea of aestheticism and the beauty of nature. Literary works exalted folk customs and historical art and encouraged spontaneity of artistic endeavor. The movement embraced the heroic ideal and the concept that heroes would raise the quality of society.

Authors who are classified as British Romantics include Samuel Taylor Coleridge, John Keats, George Byron, Mary Shelley, Percy Bysshe Shelley, and William Blake. Well-known works include Samuel Taylor Coleridge's "Kubla Khan," John Keats' "Ode on a Grecian Urn," George Byron's "Childe Harold's Pilgrimage," Mary Shelley's *Frankenstein*, Percy Bysshe Shelley's "Ode to the West Wind," and William Blake's "The Tyger."

American Romanticism

American Romanticism occurred within the American literary scene beginning early in the 19th century. While many aspects were similar to British Romanticism, it is further characterized as having gothic aspects and the idea that individualism was to be encouraged. **American Romanticism** also embraced the concept of the *noble savage*—the idea that indigenous culture uncorrupted by civilization is better than advanced society.

Well-known authors and works include Nathanial Hawthorne's *The House of the Seven Gables*, Edgar Allan Poe's "The Raven" and "The Cask of Amontillado," Emily Dickinson's "I Felt a Funeral in My Brain" and James Fenimore Cooper's *The Last of the Mohicans.*

Transcendentalism
Transcendentalism was a movement that applied to a way of thinking that developed within the United States, specifically New England, around 1836. While this way of thinking originally employed philosophical aspects, **transcendentalism** spread to all forms of art, literature, and even to the ways people chose to live. It was born out of a reaction to traditional rationalism and purported concepts such as a higher divinity, feminism, humanitarianism, and communal living. Transcendentalism valued intuition, self-reliance, and the idea that human nature was inherently good.

Well-known authors include Ralph Waldo Emerson, Henry David Thoreau, Louisa May Alcott, and Ellen Sturgis Hooper. Works include Ralph Waldo Emerson's "Self-Reliance" and "Uriel," Henry David Thoreau's *Walden* and *Civil Disobedience*, Louisa May Alcott's *Little Women*, and Ellen Sturgis Hooper's "I Slept, and Dreamed that Life was Beauty."

The Harlem Renaissance
The Harlem Renaissance is the descriptor given to the cultural, artistic, and social boom that developed in Harlem, New York, at the beginning of the 20th century, spanning the 1920s and 1930s. Originally termed *The New Negro Movement*, it emphasized African-American urban cultural expression and migration across the United States. It had strong roots in African-American Christianity, discourse, and intellectualism. The **Harlem Renaissance** heavily influenced the development of music and fashion as well. Its singular characteristic was to embrace Pan-American culturalisms; however, strong themes of the slavery experience and African-American folk traditions also emerged. A hallmark of the Harlem Renaissance was that it laid the foundation for the future Civil Rights Movement in the United States.

Well-known authors and works include Zora Neale Hurston's *Their Eyes Were Watching God*, Richard Wright's *Native Son*, Langston Hughes' "I, Too," and James Weldon Johnson's "God's Trombones: Seven Negro Sermons in Verse" and *The Book of American Negro Poetry.*

History of the Novel's Development

Eighteenth Century
The novel as it is known today first appeared in the eighteenth century. The word **novel** comes from the Italian word *novella,* which means new, referring to a new type of writing. Before this time, prose existed, but it wasn't realistic. Religion's hold over literature started to wane at this time, and authors began to write about the world around them. The novel was popularized by the use of realistic characters, set in real geographical locations and engaged in real-life situations. The earliest novels included *Robinson Crusoe* and *Moll Flanders* by Daniel Defoe. These works used the common man and woman as characters, unlike the prose that came before them, which used plots that centered on heroes, legends, and gods. Other popular novelists of this time included Jonathan Swift, Henry Fielding, and Samuel Richardson. Swift's *Gulliver's Travels* is considered an early version of the fantasy novel. The novel also flourished at this time with the growth of the printing industry. Books were readily available, and for the first time, the middle class was able to afford them. Many of the readers of these realistic stories were women. Writers took this into account and created characters that represented a wider range of people, including women and the middle class. For example, in the late eighteenth century,

Jane Austen's books were populated with female characters, and Defoe's books centered on the common man. Another development that aided the popularity of novels in the eighteenth century was the creation of libraries. The ability to borrow books made literature much more widely available to lower classes, and novels flourished in this environment.

Nineteenth Century

The trend in nineteenth-century novels was again realism. Characters and settings were realistic, and they encountered realistic situations. Some of the most important and critically acclaimed novelists come out of this era, including Jane Austen, Charles Dickens, and the Bronte sisters. Austen's novels such as *Pride and Prejudice* and *Sense and Sensibility* were extremely popular and dealt with the issue of women and their dependence on marriage in the nineteenth century for social status and economic standing. Dickens' work focused on the people of London in the Victorian age. He used realistic characters and injected humor into his works, such as *Great Expectations* and *Oliver Twist.*

In America, writers like Nathaniel Hawthorne and Mark Twain were crafting the great American novel. Twain's *Adventures of Huckleberry Finn* and Hawthorne's *The Scarlet Letter* are revered as some of the best novels of all time, each making social commentary on the American experience. Hawthorne's work in particular featured the people of Puritan New England. His work often made social commentary on his anti-Puritan views. Hawthorne was considered part of a dark Romantic movement, focusing on themes of intense emotion such as horror, apprehension, and awe. Edgar Allan Poe was also part of the Romantic movement, and his novels included these same themes, particularly horror.

Twentieth Century

The novel continued its popularity in the twentieth century. Novelists such as George Orwell, James Joyce, F. Scott Fitzgerald, Ernest Hemingway, John Steinbeck, Edith Wharton, Toni Morrison, and Franz Kafka developed novels that are still read in high school classrooms all over the world. Varying subtypes of the novel developed at this time as well. Because of the great number of novels being written, they could be classified into categories such as romance, science fiction, mystery, fantasy, and historical fiction. The science fiction novel was even further popularized by authors such as George Orwell and H. G. Wells. Readers loved this new type of novel, and Wells' *War of the Worlds* was famously read on the radio in 1938, sparking fear in listeners that it was an actual news report of an invasion by Martians.

The first part of the century focused on modernism in literature, which centered more on the decline in civilization. Authors such as D. H. Lawrence and James Joyce wrote modernist novels, with Joyce's *Ulysses* being a prime example. Virginia Woolf, along with her husband, Leonard Woolf, established the Hogarth Press, which printed her own books as well as works by T. S. Eliot. Woolf's works, such as *Mrs. Dalloway* and *To the Lighthouse,* were experimental in form, and she is considered the foremost lyrical novelist of her time. Other authors were developing their own type of novels with writers like Agatha Christie popularizing the mystery novel in the 1930s.

The world was profoundly changed by World War I and World War II, and this can be seen in the novels of the second half of the twentieth century. Postwar novelists were from many different backgrounds as a reflection of the changes in the world after the war. They were the children of immigrants in America, and authors such as Truman Capote and Tennessee Williams are homosexual or bisexual. Many novelists wrote about World War II and its impact, such as Norman Mailer's critically acclaimed *The Naked and the Dead*, published in 1948. Mailer used journalistic style in his account of the lives of a platoon of soldiers stationed in the Pacific during World War II. Joseph Heller's *Catch 22,* written after his own experience as a bombardier in the US Air Force, took a more satirical approach to the war and is considered an example of dark surrealism. Postwar novels were also influenced by the Beat movement, with Jack Kerouac's *On the Road* being one of the prime examples of this movement.

<u>Twenty-First Century</u>
The twenty-first century saw a blurring of the lines of fiction. Novelists tended to cross genres, combining the elements of romance, fantasy, science fiction, and mystery into one book. The Young Adult category was created and gained much popularity with adult readers. An example of this is the Harry Potter series by J. K. Rowling. These novels cannot be confined to a category, as they contain elements of mystery, fantasy, and romance. They were also intended for young adults but were widely read by both children and adults alike. Another important development was the advancement of the graphic novel, which combines art along with the narrative. More than a comic book, the first graphic novel was published in the late twentieth century, but it became more widely published in the twenty-first century. Graphic novels are written in many genres, but supernatural themes are widely used. The so-called death of print also has an effect on the novel as e-books and e-readers become available.

The Short Story

The short story is a work of prose fiction that is typically much shorter than a novel. It is meant to be read in one sitting. Because of its length, the short story focuses on just one plot, with a single main character, central theme, and minimal secondary characters. There is no set length of a short story, though they are typically between one thousand and twenty thousand words. The idea of a short story dates back to the time of oral traditions such as fables, parables, and fairy tales. The father of the modern American short story is said to be Edgar Allan Poe. His works are widely used as an example of the short story. Other important short story writers include Ernest Hemingway, James Joyce, and Joyce Carol Oates.

The structure of the short story is similar to that of a novel, but it differs in that a novel may contain multiple themes, plots, or characters, and a short story typically contains just one of each. The short story focuses on a single main character who faces a challenge. The plot of the short story is the arrangement of the events. Many short story authors use a chronological order of events, telling the story from beginning to end in the order that it happened. Other authors break from this chronological order using devices such as flashback. Telling the events out of order can have an effect on the writing, creating suspense or allowing the reader to have knowledge of a later event throughout the story. An example of flashback would be revealing the ending at the beginning of the story. The effect might be to show that the journey is more important than the destination. Short stories usually contain a singular central theme. The theme is the overall idea that an author wants to convey. It can also be considered a lesson in some short stories. Setting is where and when a short story takes place. Setting can refer to time of day, time of year, or time in history. Other elements, such as the author's point of view, symbolism, and imagery, are important elements to the structure of a short story.

History of the Short Story's Development

<u>Middle Ages</u>
Like the poetry of the Middle Ages, fiction was also influenced by religion. While the short story wasn't actually called this, it did exist in some forms. At this time, it was more like a tale than the formal short story format of today. These tales were a reflection of the norms of the cultures that created them. The most notable form was written by author Geoffrey Chaucer. His *Canterbury Tales* is a collection of short narrative works about a group of Pilgrims on a journey from London to Canterbury Cathedral. This work is well loved for its vivid characters and is widely accepted as a predecessor to the modern short story.

The Canterbury Tales is also significant because it was one of the first major works of literature written in the English language. After this time, works of short fiction saw a decline in the seventeenth and eighteenth centuries in favor of other types of literature.

Nineteenth Century

The modern short story as it's known today was created in the nineteenth century. Short story writers emerged in both Europe and America. Perhaps the most famous of these writers was Edgar Allan Poe. Poe's tales of horror such as "The Telltale Heart" and "The Cask of Amontillado" included all the elements of the modern short story, such as a single main character or narrator, a limited setting, and a singular central theme. Another subgenre that emerged at this time was southern gothic writing, which centered on the American South. The characters in these stories were deeply flawed and even disturbed. Rural communities were often the setting in the works of authors such as William Faulkner and Flannery O'Connor. O'Connor's "Good Country People" is an example of a southern gothic story, set in rural Georgia, populated by the common people of the South. O'Connor used this setting to make social commentary on the lack of vision or knowledge of these people.

Other important short story writers from this time included Nathaniel Hawthorne, Mark Twain, and Guy de Maupassant. Modernism was an important literary movement in the late nineteenth century, and the short story was influenced by it. Examples of the modernist movement can be seen in Anton Chekhov's "Gusev," the story of discharged soldiers dying of consumption. The late nineteenth century also included more women authors, and works by Charlotte Perkins Gilman and Kate Chopin were published. Kate Chopin wrote important short stories about women's issues, such as independence and their reliance on marriage for status. Chopin's most popular works include "Paul's Case," "Desiree's Baby," and "The Story of an Hour."

Twentieth Century

The short story continued to gain popularity in the twentieth century. Many writers of poems, plays, and novels also began to produce short stories. Writers such as Ernest Hemingway, William Faulkner, D. H. Lawrence, Kate Chopin, and James Joyce published short stories in addition to their other works at this time. Short story writers found a forum for their work in magazine format. This was the perfect way to deliver these short narratives to readers. Writers often found they could finance their larger projects such as novels and plays by selling short stories to magazines. Herman Melville said that he hated writing stories and only did so to make money.

The rise of the film industry took its toll on the short story and decreased the need for these short works. In turn, the short story also began to evolve into a new format. Writers in the nineteenth century were more concerned with plot and its resolution. In the second half of the twentieth century, short story authors began to experiment with form and often centered their stories on motifs rather than plot. Writers like Raymond Carver revived the short story a bit through this experimentation with form, and though the short story still exists today, it has never again reached the heights it did in the early part of the twentieth century.

Essays and Nonfiction

Literary Nonfiction

Nonfiction works are best characterized by their subject matter, which must be factual and real, describing true life experiences. There are several common types of literary non-fiction.

Biography

A biography is a work written about a real person (historical or currently living). It involves factual accounts of the person's life, often in a re-telling of those events based on available, researched factual information. The re-telling and dialogue, especially if related within quotes, must be accurate and reflect reliable sources. A **biography** reflects the time and place in which the person lived, with the goal of creating an understanding of the person and his/her human experience. Examples of well-known biographies include *The Life of Samuel Johnson* by James Boswell and *Steve Jobs* by Walter Isaacson.

Autobiography

An autobiography is a factual account of a person's life written by that person. It may contain some or all of the same elements as a biography, but the author is the subject matter. An **autobiography** will be told in first person narrative. Examples of well-known autobiographies in literature include *Night* by Elie Wiesel and *Margaret Thatcher: The Autobiography* by Margaret Thatcher.

Memoir

A memoir is a historical account of a person's life and experiences written by one who has personal, intimate knowledge of the information. The line between memoir, autobiography, and biography is often muddled, but generally speaking, a memoir covers a specific timeline of events as opposed to the other forms of nonfiction. A **memoir** is less all-encompassing. It is also less formal in tone and tends to focus on the emotional aspect of the presented timeline of events. Some examples of memoirs in literature include *Angela's Ashes* by Frank McCourt and *All Creatures Great and Small* by James Herriot.

Journalism

Some forms of **journalism** can fall into the category of literary non-fiction—e.g., travel writing, nature writing, sports writing, the interview, and sometimes, the essay. Some examples include Elizabeth Kolbert's "The Lost World, in the Annals of Extinction series for *The New Yorker* and Gary Smith's "Ali and His Entourage" for *Sports Illustrated*.

The Essay

An essay is a short piece of nonfiction writing. It typically uses the opinion of the author on a single subject. Essay authors can write about virtually any subject, as there are no rules for the content of an essay. It is often used to convey a point about a subject but can also be written simply for pleasure. **Essays** can make use of different writing modes, such as argument, persuasion, causal analysis, critique, or observation. They can be formal or informal, serious in tone, satirical, or even humorous. Organization is up to the author and does not follow any strict rules. Virginia Woolf wrote a series of essays, most notably about the struggle for survival in her essay "Death of a Moth." George Orwell's essay "Shooting an Elephant" includes his graphic account of shooting an elephant as social commentary on anti-colonialism.

The Speech

A speech is a formal address meant to be spoken aloud to an audience. The purpose of a speech can vary but is typically to persuade, argue, inform, or inspire the audience. **Speeches** can be political in nature but don't have to be. Some of the most famous speeches include Martin Luther King's "I Have a Dream" speech, Abraham Lincoln's Gettysburg Address, and John F. Kennedy's inaugural address. Some important components of a speech are the style, substance, and impact of the words. While the writing of a speech is important, the delivery is important as well.

Speeches can be delivered in four methods: **impromptu**, with little to no preparation; **extemporaneous**, which involves preparation but is not read directly from cards; **manuscript**, which is read directly from a script or teleprompter; and **memorized**, which is a written speech delivered from the speaker's memory. The speech delivery type depends on the situation and reaction a speaker wants from the audience. Extemporaneous speaking is the most common delivery method, and many great speakers have used this format because it appears more natural to the audience. It is widely known that Martin Luther King's "I Have a Dream" speech was delivered extemporaneously, as he largely improvised the second half of the speech, including the portion where he states, "I have a dream." George W. Bush's Bullhorn speech, delivered at ground zero on September 14, 2001, in the wake of the September 11 terror attacks, is an example of an impromptu speech. Though he had not planned to speak at the event and was even advised against it, Bush took a bullhorn and spoke to the crowd, aiming to lift the spirits of a broken nation, delivering a memorable impromptu speech.

Literary Theory

A **literary theory** can be considered a methodology for understanding literature. It asks, "What is literature?" and offers readers a working set of principles to understand common themes, ideas, and intent. Classifications of literary theory are often referred to as *schools of thought*. These schools are based on subdivisions in historical perspective and in philosophical thinking across literary analysts and critics.

Romanticism/Aestheticism
Romanticism/Aestheticism spanned the 19th century and developed in response to the idea that enlightenment and reason were the source of all truth and authority in philosophy. **Romanticism** and **Aestheticism** embraced the tenet that *aesthetics*—all that is beautiful and natural—in art and literature should be considered the highest-held principle, overriding all others. Popular authors include Oscar Wilde, Edgar Allan Poe, Mary Shelley, and John Keats.

Marxism
Marxism as a literary theory developed in the early twentieth century after the Russian October Revolution of 1917. It loosely embraced the idea that social realism was the highest form of literature and that the social classes' struggle for progress was the most important concept literature could emphasize. Examples of authors include Simone de Beauvoir and Bertolt Brecht.

Structuralism
Structuralism included all aspects of philosophy, linguistics, anthropology, and literary theory. Beginning in the early 1900s, this school of thought focused on ideas surrounding how human culture is understood within its larger structures and how those structures influence people's thoughts and actions. Specifically, structuralism examines how literature is interconnected through structure. It examines common elements in the stories and the myths that contribute to literature as a whole. Popular theorists and writers include Claude Levi-Strauss, Umberto Eco, and Roland Barthes.

Post-Structuralism and Deconstruction
Post-Structuralism and deconstruction developed out of structuralism in the twentieth century. It expanded on the idea of overall structure in literature, but both theories argue varying analytical concepts of how that structure should be examined and utilized. For example, while structuralism acknowledges oppositional relationships in literature—e.g., male/female, beginning/end, rational/emotional—**post-structuralism** and **deconstruction** began de-emphasizing the idea that one idea is always dominant over another. Both also assert that studying text also means studying the knowledge that produced the text. Popular theorists and writers include Roland Barthes and Michel Foucault.

New Criticism

New Criticism dominated American culture in the mid-twentieth century. It purports that close, critical reading was necessary to understanding literary works, especially poetry. Popular theory also focused on the inherent beauty of text itself. **New Criticism** rejected the previous critical focus of how history, use of language, and the author's experience influence literature, asserting those ideas as being too loosely interpretive in examining literature. As a movement, it tended to separate literature from historical context and an author's intent. It embraced the idea that formal study of structure and text should not be separated. Theorists of note include Stephen Greenblatt and Jonathan Goldberg.

Poetry

The genre of **poetry** refers to literary works that focus on the expression of feelings and ideas through the use of structure and linguistic rhythm to create a desired effect.

Different poetic structures and devices are used to create the various major forms of poetry. Some of the most common forms are discussed in the following chart.

Type	Poetic Structure	Example
Ballad	A poem or song passed down orally which tells a story and in English tradition usually uses an ABAB or ABCB rhyme scheme	William Butler Yeats' "The Ballad Of Father O'Hart"
Epic	A long poem from ancient oral tradition which narrates the story of a legendary or heroic protagonist	Homer's The Odyssey Virgil's The Aeneid
Haiku	A Japanese poem of three unrhymed lines with five, seven, and five syllables (in English) with nature as a common subject matter	Matsuo Bashō An old silent pond... A frog jumps into the pond, splash! Silence again.
Limerick	A five-line poem written in an AABBA rhyme scheme, with a witty focus	From Edward Lear's Book of Nonsense— "There was a Young Person of Smyrna Whose grandmother threatened to burn her..."
Ode	A formal lyric poem that addresses and praises a person, place, thing, or idea	Edna St. Vincent Millay's "Ode To Silence"
Sonnet	A fourteen-line poem written in iambic pentameter	Shakespeare's Sonnets 18 and 130

Understanding Poetic Devices and Structure

Poetic Devices
Rhyme is the poet's use of corresponding word sounds in order to create an effect. Most rhyme occurs at the ends of a poem's lines, which is how readers arrive at the **rhyme scheme**. Each line that has a corresponding rhyming sound is assigned a letter—A, B, C, and so on. When using a rhyme scheme,

poets will often follow lettered patterns. Robert Frost's *"The Road Not Taken"* uses the ABAAB rhyme scheme:

Two roads diverged in a yellow wood,	A
And sorry I could not travel both	B
And be one traveler, long I stood	A
And looked down one as far as I could	A
To where it bent in the undergrowth;	B

Another important poetic device is **rhythm**—metered patterns within poetry verses. When a poet develops rhythm through **meter**, he or she is using a combination of stressed and unstressed syllables to create a sound effect for the reader.

Rhythm is created by the use of poetic feet—individual rhythmic units made up of the combination of stressed and unstressed syllables. A line of poetry is made up of one or more poetic feet. There are five standard types in English poetry, as depicted in the chart below.

Foot Type	Rhythm	Pattern
Iamb	buh Buh	Unstressed/stressed
Trochee	Buh buh	Stressed/unstressed
Spondee	Buh Buh	Stressed/stressed
Anapest	buh buh Buh	Unstressed/unstressed/stressed
Dactyl	Buh buh buh	Stressed/unstressed/unstressed

Structure

Poetry is most easily recognized by its structure, which varies greatly. For example, a structure may be strict in the number of lines it uses. It may use rhyming patterns or may not rhyme at all. There are three main types of poetic structures:

- *Verse*—poetry with a consistent meter and rhyme scheme
- *Blank verse*—poetry with consistent meter but an inconsistent rhyme scheme
- *Free verse*—poetry with inconsistent meter or rhyme

Verse poetry is most often developed in the form of **stanzas**—groups of word lines. Stanzas can also be considered *verses*. The structure is usually formulaic and adheres to the protocols for the form. For example, the English sonnet form uses a structure of fourteen lines and a variety of different rhyming patterns. The English ode typically uses three ten-line stanzas and has a particular rhyming pattern.

Poets choose poetic structure based on the effect they want to create. Some structures—such as the ballad and haiku—developed out of cultural influences and common artistic practice in history, but in more modern poetry, authors choose their structure to best fit their intended effect.

History of Poetry's Development

Ancient Times

Poetry has been in existence for thousands of years and can be considered to predate literacy. Early poems were passed on through oral tradition, rather than written, and sung or recited as a way to remember a culture's history. The ancient Greek poets were the first to commit their poetry to the written format in the seventh to fourth century BC. The Greeks often wrote poetry about their gods.

Greek poetry took three forms: epic, lyric, and dramatic. It used meter, and Greeks were the first to introduce iambic pentameter. Some of the greatest poets of this time included Homer, Aeschylus, and Euripides. Homer's *The Iliad* and *The Odyssey,* which focused on Greek mythology, are two of the most famous epic poems from this time period. Lyric poets of ancient Greece included Alcaeus, Sappho, and Pindar. Sappho was a female poet from the island of Lesbos. Most of her poetry exists in fragments, though her most complete poem, "Ode to Aphrodite," is influenced by and makes references to Homer's *The Iliad.* The dramatic poetry of ancient Greece was written by Aeschylus and Sophocles, among others. It was divided into the same categories seen today in modern drama of tragedy and comedy.

When Greece was conquered by the Romans, their works were borrowed and adapted and eventually became the basis for modern literature. Romans wrote in Latin, and the Greek influence is clear in their poetry. Some of the oldest Roman literature is actually a translation of Greek works. Greco-Roman poet Andronicus first translated Homer's *The Odyssey* from Greek into Latin for a Roman audience. Though this was done for educational purposes at first, it became the basis for more Roman works and helped to develop Roman literature. Ovid was one of the most famous Roman poets. He is best known for *Metamorphoses,* a narrative poem consisting of fifteen texts. It spans the history of the world in myths from creation to the time of Julius Caesar and is one of the most influential texts in poetry to date. Another of Rome's great poets, Virgil, is best known for his *Aeneid.* This epic poem, written between 29 BC and 19 BC, tells the story of mythological Trojan hero Aeneas and his journey to Italy.

Middle Ages to Seventeenth Century

Poems in the Middle Ages were influenced by the historical events of the time, including religious movements. They were often religious in nature and typically written in Latin, as this was the predominant language of the Roman Catholic Church. Geoffrey Chaucer, a famous medieval writer, experimented with using the vernacular, or common, language of the people, writing works such as *The Parliament of Birds* and *The Canterbury Tales* in English. *Beowulf,* written by an anonymous Anglo-Saxon poet, is probably the most well-known poem to come out of the medieval period. It is an epic written in Old English, the vernacular language of the time. While its origins are unknown, this is the first time *Beowulf* was taken from oral tradition to written format.

The Renaissance brought with it one of the most prolific times in poetry's history. This cultural movement saw creative advancements in literature, art, and music, lasting from the fifteenth to the seventeenth century. Some of the most famous poetry to come from this time period includes William Shakespeare's sonnets. During the Enlightenment period that followed, there was a return to the style of the ancient Greeks, with a concentration on the epic poem. Alexander Pope was the most famous poet of this time, known for his satirical works and the use of the heroic couplet. The end of the eighteenth century brought about the birth of Romanticism and such famous British poets as William Blake, Lord Byron, William Wordsworth, and John Keats. Many of these poets got their inspiration from the natural world, which was in contrast to the religious themes in the poetry that came before it.

Nineteenth Century

Romanticism carried over into the nineteenth century, when there was also a rise in American poetry. These early American poets, as they became known, included Walt Whitman, Robert Frost, and Henry Wadsworth Longfellow. Whitman, specifically, was known as the father of free verse, and his works helped to set American poets apart from their British counterparts. Most of these poets were known as transcendentalists, focusing on themes of spirituality, nature, and utopian values. Whitman's *Leaves of Grass*, published in 1855, was his idea of an American epic. The poetry in *Leaves of Grass* does not rhyme or follow any specific metric pattern. Its themes of sensual pleasures of the body and the natural world were novel and controversial at this time, and it has become one of the most influential works by an American poet.

Poetry of the nineteenth century also saw more working-class themes and authors from working-class backgrounds. This poetry had its roots in politics, rather than religion, nature, or romantic themes. This was also an important time for women in poetry, with the works of Emily Dickinson, Emily Bronte, and Elizabeth Browning gaining popularity. Dickinson's lyric poems used short lines, unconventional spelling and punctuation, and often lacked titles. While she wrote hundreds of poems in her lifetime, because of its unconventional style, most of Dickinson's work was published after her death. Her "Because I Could Not Stop for Death," published posthumously in 1890, exemplified her unique and influential style of meter and rhyme. Modernist poetry also got its start in the late nineteenth century. This format is marked by a movement from the personal to the world around the individual. It was born in the nineteenth century but flourished in the early twentieth century.

Twentieth Century

Modernist poetry continued into the twentieth century, with poets such as T. S. Eliot, Ezra Pound, and Gertrude Stein. Modernist poetry is characterized by the use of allusion and fragmented language. Some other smaller movements that grew out of modernism include free verse, Dadaism, and surrealism. The twentieth century also saw the rise in African American poets with the Harlem Renaissance spanning the 1920s and 1930s. The publishing industry sought out African American writers whose poetry focused on a realistic portrayal of their lives. One of the most important writers to come out of this movement was Langston Hughes, whose poetry depicted an honest portrayal of his life and struggles as a black man living in America.

Another important poetry movement of the twentieth century was the Beat movement, which lasted from 1948 to 1963. Beat poetry, born out of New York and San Francisco, was characterized by anti-conformist themes and influenced by ideas of sexual freedom and drug use. Some of the most famous Beat poets include Allen Ginsberg and Lawrence Ferlinghetti, whose works challenged the social norms of the time. The second half of the twentieth century saw the advent of confessional poetry with the works of Sylvia Plath. Her poetry was deeply personal and rooted in natural themes in a lyrical style. Near the end of the nineteenth century, the New Formalism movement brought back the meter and rhyme of more traditional poetry. Poets such as Charles Martin, Brad Leithauser, and Molly Peacock adopted this New Formalist style.

Twenty-First Century

Contemporary poetry can take many forms and abides by no strict rules. Poets of the twenty-first century write about anything, from technology to love to civil rights. Their poetry tends to be more realistic in nature, and liberties are taken with form and structure. Poets of the twenty-first century often inject humor into their poetry and do not take the form quite as seriously as those that came before them. Sherman Alexie, for example, writes often about the plight of Native Americans but does so using irony and dark humor. Rita Dove, a poet laureate to both the state of Virginia and the Library of

Congress, is another important twenty-first-century poet. Her work often has a historical aspect and uses themes from other art forms, such as music and dance. Dove's *Sonata Mullatica*, published in 2009, is a collection of poetry about the life of George Bridgetower, a biracial musician from the seventeenth century, and his friendship with Beethoven. Poetry in the twenty-first century has been affected by the digital age, and many poems are now exclusively written and published in electronic format. The Internet has created a new forum for poetry that has helped it to continue to develop into the modern age. This has given readers exposure to poetry from all over the world from poets such as Claribel Alegria of Nicaragua, Elie Rajaonarison from Madagascar, and Conceicao Lima of Sao Tome and Principe in West Africa.

Drama

Drama is a type of fiction that is based on a script that is meant to be performed. Works of drama are called **plays**. Plays are intended to be performed on a stage by actors in front of an audience. Like other works of fiction, plays contain characters, plot, setting, theme, symbolism, and imagery. The main difference is that plays are sectioned into acts and scenes rather than chapters or stanzas. Drama is one of the oldest forms of literature, and it has evolved from the first Greek tragedies, such as *Antigone* and *Prometheus Bound*, into what is performed on modern stages today.

Like prose fiction, drama has several genres. The following are the most common ones:

- Comedy: a humorous play designed to amuse and entertain, often with an emphasis on the common person's experience, generally resolved in a positive way—e.g., Richard Sheridan's *School for Scandal*, Shakespeare's *Taming of the Shrew*, Neil Simon's *The Odd Couple*

- History: a play based on recorded history where the fate of a nation or kingdom is at the core of the conflict—e.g., Christopher Marlowe's *Edward II*, Shakespeare's *King Richard III*, Arthur Miller's *The Crucible*

- Tragedy: a serious play that often involves the downfall of the protagonist. In modern tragedies, the protagonist is not necessarily in a position of power or authority—e.g., Jean Racine's *Phèdre*, Arthur Miller's *Death of a Salesman*, John Steinbeck's *Of Mice and Men*

- Melodrama: a play that emphasizes heightened emotion and sensationalism, generally with stereotypical characters in exaggerated or realistic situations and with moral polarization—e.g., Jean-Jacques Rousseau's *Pygmalion*

- Tragi-comedy: a play that has elements of both tragedy—a character experiencing a tragic loss—and comedy—the resolution is often positive with no clear distinctive mood for either—e.g., Shakespeare's *The Merchant of Venice*, Anton Chekhov's *The Cherry Orchard*

Structural Elements

The text of the play is called a **script**, and it is made up of both stage directions and dialogue. Stage directions are sections of the play that set the scene. Set directions might include information on what the scenery should look like and where the actors should stand. Plays also contain **dialogue**, which refers to the actual words the actors should speak. The difference in a play and other literary forms is in its construction and that it is intended to be performed. Plays are typically made up of acts. A playwright might use acts to indicate a change in time, setting, or mood. Acts can also be divided into scenes. A scene change may be used to indicate a change in the action, to introduce new characters, or to indicate a change in setting at the same time. In a play, there may be a protagonist, or central character, and an antagonist, who opposes the protagonist. A play, like fictional prose, often uses the following plot structure known as dramatic structure or Freytag's pyramid: exposition, rising action, climax, falling action, and denouement.

- *Exposition*—The first part of the play that introduces background information about setting, characters, plot, backstories, etc.
- *Rising action*—A series of events that build up to the main event of the story

- *Climax*—The main event or turning point of the play, when things turn around for a protagonist in a comedy or start to go bad for the protagonist in a tragedy
- *Falling action*—The part when the plot slows down and starts moving toward a conclusion; often the logical consequence of the climax
- *Denouement*—The ending of the play when conflicts are resolved

A longer play may also contain subplots, which are secondary or in contrast to the main plot. A play can have one or more themes, depending on its length.

As an example, the following dramatic structure is used in Shakespeare's *Romeo and Juliet*:

Exposition: The setting of Verona, Italy; protagonists Romeo and Juliet are introduced; and the feud between the Capulets and the Montagues is revealed.

Rising action: Romeo and Juliet meet and fall in love but cannot be together because of the feud.

Climax: Juliet's cousin Tybalt kills Mercutio, igniting the feud. Romeo kills Tybalt and is banished. Romeo and Juliet two secretly marry.

Falling action: Juliet fakes her death to avoid an arranged marriage and be with Romeo; Romeo plans his own suicide when he learns she has (seemingly) died.

Denouement: Romeo commits suicide at Juliet's tomb. She wakes to find him dead and also commits suicide. When the families learn they were secretly married, they resolve to end their long-standing feud.

History of Drama's Development

Ancient Times
The ancient Greeks are widely accepted as the inventors of drama. The word *drama* comes from the Greek word meaning action. The earliest plays were religious in nature, focusing on the Greek gods. Greek drama included comedy, which was satirical and made light of the foils of men in power. The Greek tragedies were a bit more involved, including themes of love and loss. They typically involved the downfall of the protagonist, an otherwise good person, because of a fatal flaw. For example, in Sophocles' *Antigone*, the title character's tragic flaw is her loyalty to the gods.

Greek drama also included a chorus, masked performers who represent the voice of society. They spoke in unison and offered commentary on the dramatic action of the play. The chorus also sang, danced, and recited poetry during the play. Important playwrights of this time included Aeschylus, Sophocles, and Euripides. These early Greek playwrights greatly influenced the writers who came after them, with Aeschylus being called the father of modern drama. Aeschylus' *Oresteia* is likely the first example of a play in trilogy format. Other important works of this time included Sophocles' *Antigone* and *Oedipus Rex*, Euripides' *Medea*, and Aeschylus' *Prometheus Bound*.

Middle Ages
In the Middle Ages, drama continued to be influenced by religion. Three types of drama began to emerge in the medieval period: mystery play, miracle play, and morality play. The **mystery play** focused on biblical stories. These plays contained multiple acts and were performed by religious figures such as priests or monks. The **miracle play**, also with a religious theme, focused on the life of a saint. The **morality play** was meant to teach the audience a lesson based on the rules of the church. Two kinds of

stages were invented for medieval drama: the fixed stage and the movable stage. While there were some comic elements to medieval plays, their religious nature made them mostly serious in tone. Secular plays were less popular at this time but did exist, particularly in France, where the farce was typically performed by professional actors in public forums.

Renaissance

The Renaissance was a prolific time for drama. This time period gave birth to the Elizabethan drama, popularized by playwrights such as Ben Jonson, Christopher Marlowe, and William Shakespeare. Shakespeare wrote both drama and comedy, and his plays such as *Romeo and Juliet, Hamlet, Macbeth,* and many more are some of the most recognized and acclaimed plays of all time. He also popularized a new type of drama, the romantic play, which did not fit in either of the previous categories. Elizabethan drama saw a break from the religious themes of the plays that came before it and a shift in focus from God to people. Like in the Greek tragedies before them, the tragedies of this period were marked by a protagonist with a central flaw, which ultimately brings him to his downfall.

An important development during this period was the establishment of permanent theaters. These large theaters were profitable and gave playwrights a designated place to showcase their plays. Having designated theaters allowed the creation of theater companies made up of common men, and young boys often played the roles of women. Women were not allowed to act in plays until after 1660, as it was not deemed a suitable profession for them. Queen Elizabeth I loved drama and was a patron of Shakespeare. Her interest in and support for the theater helped it to flourish during her reign.

Seventeenth and Eighteenth Centuries

The Elizabethan playwrights continued to develop plays in the seventeenth century, but the Puritanical government of the mid-seventeenth century shut down theaters for a time. When King Charles II came into power in 1660, the theater ban was lifted. Theaters once again flourished after the English Restoration. Women were now able to perform in these dramas, bringing life to the intended female roles, with Margaret Hughes credited as the first female actress in English theater. This time period also saw the first recognized female playwright, Aphra Behn. Her two-part play, *The Rover*, was written in 1677. New types of drama that were developed at this time included heroic drama and Restoration comedy, which made use of immoral themes. The eighteenth century saw the fall of Restoration comedy and the rise of musical comedies and themes much more geared to musical entertainment than serious drama. John Gay's *The Beggar's Opera*, for example, was written to the tune of popular music of the time.

Nineteenth Century to the Present

In the nineteenth century, drama was influenced by the Victorian era. **Closet drama**, a type of dramatic play that is meant to be read rather than performed, became more popular. As for the stage, melodrama became very popular at this time. Melodrama used music to enhance the more dramatic scenes of plays. Shorter musical acts were also included in nineteenth-century productions and often interspersed between acts of plays. Toward the end of the nineteenth century, modernist plays such as Henrik Ibsen's *A Doll's House,* written in 1879, tackled such issues as the emancipation of women. Russian playwright Anton Chekhov also wrote modernist plays at this time. His works were unique in that the most meaningful parts of the play were not in the words but in the set direction for the actors. In the early twentieth century, playwrights such as T. S. Eliot and American playwrights such as Arthur Miller and Tennessee Williams saw their plays not only produced for the stage, but also the screen. The advent of television and film created a new format and a wider audience for these dramatic plays. Miller's *Death of a Salesman* and *The Crucible* were made into television and motion picture films, respectively. Williams' *A Streetcar Named Desire* was made into a major motion picture that went on to win four Academy Awards. More recent contemporary playwrights such as David Mamet often write both stage plays and screenplays for films. Mamet has won the Pulitzer Prize for his dramatic plays *Speed-the-Plow* and *Glengarry Glen Ross* and earned Oscar nominations for his screenplays.

Practice Questions

Questions 1 through 10 refer to the following passage:

ACT II SCENE II

Capulet's orchard.

[Enter ROMEO]

ROMEO   He jests at scars that never felt a wound.

[JULIET appears above at a window]

But, soft! what light through yonder window breaks?

It is the east, and Juliet is the sun.

Arise, fair sun, and kill the envious moon,

Who is already sick and pale with grief,

That thou her maid art far more fair than she:

Be not her maid, since she is envious;

Her vestal livery is but sick and green

And none but fools do wear it; cast it off.

It is my lady, O, it is my love!   10

O, that she knew she were!

She speaks yet she says nothing: what of that?

Her eye discourses; I will answer it.

I am too bold, 'tis not to me she speaks:

Two of the fairest stars in all the heaven,

Having some business, do entreat her eyes

To twinkle in their spheres till they return.

What if her eyes were there, they in her head?

The brightness of her cheek would shame those stars,

As daylight doth a lamp; her eyes in heaven   20

	Would through the airy region stream so bright	
	That birds would sing and think it were not night.	
	See, how she leans her cheek upon her hand!	
	O, that I were a glove upon that hand,	
	That I might touch that cheek!	
JULIET	Ay me!	
ROMEO	She speaks:	
	O, speak again, bright angel! for thou art	
	As glorious to this night, being o'er my head	
	As is a winged messenger of heaven	
	Unto the white-upturned wondering eyes	
	Of mortals that fall back to gaze on him	30
	When he bestrides the lazy-pacing clouds	
	And sails upon the bosom of the air.	
JULIET	O Romeo, Romeo! wherefore art thou Romeo?	
	Deny thy father and refuse thy name;	
	Or, if thou wilt not, be but sworn my love,	
	And I'll no longer be a Capulet.	
ROMEO	*[Aside]* Shall I hear more, or shall I speak at this?	
JULIET	'Tis but thy name that is my enemy;	
	Thou art thyself, though not a Montague.	
	What's Montague? it is nor hand, nor foot,	40
	Nor arm, nor face, nor any other part	
	Belonging to a man. O, be some other name!	
	What's in a name? that which we call a rose	
	By any other name would smell as sweet;	
	So Romeo would, were he not Romeo call'd,	

Retain that dear perfection which he owes

Without that title. Romeo, doff thy name,

And for that name which is no part of thee

Take all myself.

1. In the passage that begins, "What's Montague? It is nor hand, nor foot, / Nor arm, nor face, nor any other part...," what is Juliet essentially saying?
    a. That she isn't special
    b. That Romeo shouldn't care about her
    c. That his name means they cannot be together
    d. That she would love Romeo no matter what his name is
    e. That her name is more important than his

2. Which statement best describes Romeo's intent when he says the moon is envious?
    a. The sun is rising.
    b. The sun and stars are shining.
    c. Juliet is more beautiful.
    d. The moon is sick.
    e. The moon is paler than the sun.

3. Which of the following describes the tone of lines 10 through 25?
    a. Desirous
    b. Remorseful
    c. Respectful
    d. Tentative
    e. Hesitant

4. Which of the following lines indicates the famous balcony scene from the play?
    a. "And sails upon the bosom of the air."
    b. "Two of the fairest stars in all the heaven,"
    c. "As glorious to this night, being o'er my head"
    d. "He jests at scars that never felt a wound."
    e. "When he bestrides the lazy-pacing clouds"

5. The line, "As glorious to this night, being o'er my head / As is a winged messenger of heaven," is an example of which of the following?
    a. Metaphor
    b. Simile
    c. Personification
    d. Imagery
    e. Theme

6. Which of the following is an example of imagery?
    a. "Thou art thyself, though not a Montague."
    b. "O, that I were a glove upon that hand,"
    c. "I am too bold, 'tis not to me she speaks:"
    d. "Deny thy father and refuse thy name;"
    e. "That birds would sing and think it were not night."

7. Which of the following is an example of personification?
    a. "Without that title. Romeo, doff thy name,"
    b. "I am too bold, 'tis not to me she speaks:"
    c. "O, speak again, bright angel!"
    d. "Arise, fair sun, and kill the envious moon,"
    e. "And I'll no longer be a Capulet."

8. Which of the following best describes the overall theme of this passage?
    a. Nature is more important than love.
    b. Love is stronger than death.
    c. Love will conquer all.
    d. Young people in love are foolish.
    e. Women are more beautiful than nature.

9. In the context of the poem, the line, "She speaks yet she says nothing: what of that? / Her eye discourses; I will answer it," can best be restated as which of the following?
    a. Juliet doesn't say anything, but her beauty speaks for her.
    b. Juliet speaks to Romeo, but he can't hear her.
    c. Romeo is speechless because of her beauty.
    d. Romeo wants to speak to Juliet, but he is afraid.
    e. Juliet looks at Romeo but says nothing.

10. With the final two lines of the passage, what does Juliet offer?
    a. She offers herself in exchange for Romeo's name.
    b. She offers to marry Romeo so she can take his name.
    c. She offers to leave her family so they can be together.
    d. She offers her heart for his word.
    e. She offers her kingdom for his name.

Happy the man, whose wish and care

A few paternal acres bound,

Content to breathe his native air,

In his own ground.

Whose herds with milk, whose fields with bread,

Whose flocks supply him with attire,

Whose trees in summer yield him shade,

In winter fire.

Blest, who can unconcernedly find

Hours, days, and years slide soft away,

In health of body, peace of mind,

Quiet by day,

Sound sleep by night; study and ease,

Together mixed; sweet recreation;

And innocence, which most does please,

With meditation.

Thus let me live, unseen, unknown;

Thus unlamented let me die;

Steal from the world, and not a stone

Tell where I lie.

"Ode on Solitude" by Alexander Pope

11. Which of these best describes the speaker of the poem?
    a. A young girl who is lonely
    b. An old man who enjoys being alone
    c. An unnamed narrator who lists the joys of being alone
    d. A man who feels alone most of the time
    e. A lonely farmer

12. Which of the following best describes the tone of the poem?
    a. Pensive
    b. Dejected
    c. Despondent
    d. Indignant
    e. Buoyant

13. What is the meaning of the word paternal in the first stanza?
    a. The man is a father.
    b. The man works for his father.
    c. The land was passed down from his father.
    d. The land is made up of pastures.
    e. The man is standing in a field with his father.

14. What inference can be made about the speaker in the final stanza?
    a. The speaker is lonely, so he wants to die.
    b. The speaker's family is gone, so he wants his life to end.
    c. The speaker has lost his will to live.
    d. The speaker is ill and wishes to die.
    e. The speaker wishes to be left alone to live and die in peace.

15. What do the lines, "Whose herds with milk, whose fields with bread, / Whose flocks supply him with attire," suggest about the man's life?
    a. The man is very good at farming.
    b. The man's farm produces grain.
    c. The man is very busy on his farm.
    d. The man's farm provides him with everything he needs.
    e. The man's farm has cows, sheep, and crops.

16. Which type of poem is "Ode on Solitude"?
    a. A lyric poem addressed to a particular subject
    b. A song narrating a story in short stanzas
    c. A lengthy narrative poem dealing with heroic deeds
    d. A poem of serious reflection, typically on the dead
    e. A literary work dealing with rural life and its contrast to city life

17. The farm the man lives on is an example of which of the following?
    a. Imagery
    b. Theme
    c. Character
    d. Symbolism
    e. Setting

18. What realization does the main character come to at the end of the poem?
   a. He is lonely in his life on the farm.
   b. His farm has been very successful.
   c. He would like to die simply, just as he lived.
   d. He regrets his choices to live alone.
   e. He will miss his life of solitude.

19. What is the meaning of the word unlamented in the final stanza?
   a. Not mourned
   b. Alone
   c. Regret
   d. Inconsolable
   e. Not loved

20. In the fourth stanza, Pope suggests that a key to happiness is a balance of work and play. This is an example of which of the following?
   a. Imagery
   b. Theme
   c. Symbolism
   d. Setting
   e. Character

Questions 21 through 30 refer to the following passage:

Alice was beginning to get very tired of sitting by her sister on the bank, and of having nothing to do: once or twice she had peeped into the book her sister was reading, but it had no pictures or conversations in it, "and what is the use of a book," thought Alice "without pictures or conversation?"

So she was considering in her own mind (as well as she could, for the hot day made her feel very sleepy and stupid), whether the pleasure of making a daisy-chain would be worth the trouble of getting up and picking the daisies, when suddenly a White Rabbit with pink eyes ran close by her.

There was nothing so *very* remarkable in that; nor did Alice think it so *very* much out of the way to hear the Rabbit say to itself, "Oh dear! Oh dear! I shall be late!" (when she thought it over afterwards, it occurred to her that she ought to have wondered at this, but at the time it all seemed quite natural); but when the Rabbit actually *took a watch out of its waistcoat-pocket*, and looked at it, and then hurried on, Alice started to her feet, for it flashed across her mind that she had never before seen a rabbit with either a waistcoat-pocket, or a watch to take out of it, and burning with curiosity, she ran across the field after it, and fortunately was just in time to see it pop down a large rabbit-hole under the hedge.

In another moment down went Alice after it, never once considering how in the world she was to get out again.

The rabbit-hole went straight on like a tunnel for some way, and then dipped suddenly down, so suddenly that Alice had not a moment to think about stopping herself before she found herself falling down a very deep well.

Either the well was very deep, or she fell very slowly, for she had plenty of time as she went down to look about her and to wonder what was going to happen next. First, she tried to look down and make out what she was coming to, but it was too dark to see anything; then she looked at the sides of the well, and noticed that they were filled with cupboards and book-shelves; here and there she saw maps and pictures hung upon pegs. She took down a jar from one of the shelves as she passed; it was labelled "ORANGE MARMALADE," but to her great disappointment it was empty: she did not like to drop the jar for fear of killing somebody, so managed to put it into one of the cupboards as she fell past it.

"Well!" thought Alice to herself, "after such a fall as this, I shall think nothing of tumbling down stairs! How brave they'll all think me at home! Why, I wouldn't say anything about it, even if I fell off the top of the house!" (Which was very likely true.)

Down, down, down. Would the fall *never* come to an end! "I wonder how many miles I've fallen by this time?" she said aloud. "I must be getting somewhere near the centre of the earth. Let me see: that would be four thousand miles down, I think—" (for, you see, Alice had learnt several things of this sort in her lessons in the schoolroom, and though this was not a *very* good opportunity for showing off her knowledge, as there was no one to listen to her, still it was good practice to say it over) "—yes, that's about the right distance—but then I wonder what Latitude or Longitude I've got to?" (Alice had no idea what Latitude was, or Longitude either, but thought they were nice grand words to say.)

Presently she began again. "I wonder if I shall fall right *through* the earth! How funny it'll seem to come out among the people that walk with their heads downward! The Antipathies, I think—" (she was rather glad there *was* no one listening, this time, as it didn't sound at all the right word) "—but I shall have to ask them what the name of the country is, you know. Please, Ma'am, is this New Zealand or Australia?" (and she tried to curtsey as she spoke—fancy *curtseying* as you're falling through the air! Do you think you could manage it?) "And what an ignorant little girl she'll think me for asking! No, it'll never do to ask: perhaps I shall see it written up somewhere."

Down, down, down. There was nothing else to do, so Alice soon began talking again. "Dinah'll miss me very much to-night, I should think!" (Dinah was the cat.) "I hope they'll remember her saucer of milk at tea-time. Dinah my dear! I wish you were down here with me! There are no mice in the air, I'm afraid, but you might catch a bat, and that's very like a mouse, you know. But do cats eat bats, I wonder?" And here Alice began to get rather sleepy, and went on saying to herself, in a dreamy sort of way, "Do cats eat bats? Do cats eat bats?" and sometimes, "Do bats eat cats?" for, you see, as she couldn't answer either question, it didn't much matter which way she put it. She felt that she was dozing off, and had just begun to dream that she was walking hand in hand with Dinah, and saying to her very earnestly, "Now, Dinah, tell me the truth: did you ever eat a bat?" when suddenly, thump! thump! down she came upon a heap of sticks and dry leaves, and the fall was over.

Alice was not a bit hurt, and she jumped up on to her feet in a moment: she looked up, but it was all dark overhead; before her was another long passage, and the White Rabbit was still in sight, hurrying down it. There was not a moment to be lost: away went Alice like the wind, and was just in time to hear it say, as it turned a corner, "Oh my ears and whiskers, how late it's getting!" She was close behind it when she turned the corner, but the Rabbit was no longer to be seen: she found herself in a long, low hall, which was lit up by a row of lamps hanging from the roof. There were doors all round the hall, but they were all locked; and when Alice had been all the way down one side and up the other, trying every door, she walked sadly down the middle, wondering how she was ever to get out again.

Alice's Adventures in Wonderland by Lewis Carroll

21. Alice's demeanor in the opening lines of the passage can be best described as which of the following?
    a. Irritable
    b. Weary
    c. Insolent
    d. Amused
    e. Indignant

22. Carroll's description of Alice's whereabouts and her demeanor in the first lines of the passage is an example of which literary device?
    a. Euphemism
    b. Imagery
    c. Personification
    d. Exposition
    e. Metaphor

23. Regarding the length of Alice's fall, what can we say about this type of work?
    a. It is a realistic novel.
    b. It is a mystery novel.
    c. It is a fantasy novel.
    d. It is a romance novel.
    e. It is a horror novel.

24. What do the lines "…she ran across the field after it, and fortunately was just in time to see it pop down a large rabbit-hole under the hedge. In another moment down went Alice after it, never once considering how in the world she was to get out again," reveal about Alice's character?
    a. She is not very intelligent.
    b. She is curious.
    c. She is bored.
    d. She is courageous.
    e. She is insane.

25. An important theme in Alice's Adventures in Wonderland is the idea of identity and a child finding her place in the world. Which of the following lines exemplifies that theme?
    a. "'Well!' thought Alice to herself, 'after such a fall as this, I shall think nothing of tumbling down stairs! How brave they'll all think me at home!'"
    b. "There was nothing so *very* remarkable in that; nor did Alice think it so *very* much out of the way to hear the Rabbit say to itself, 'Oh dear! Oh dear! I shall be late!'"
    c. "So she was considering in her own mind (as well as she could, for the hot day made her feel very sleepy and stupid),"
    d. "Down, down, down. Would the fall *never* come to an end! 'I wonder how many miles I've fallen by this time?' she said aloud."
    e. "'I must be getting somewhere near the centre of the earth. Let me see: that would be four thousand miles down, I think—'"

26. Based on this passage, what point of view is the story told from?
    a. First person point of view from Alice's perspective
    b. First person point of view with an unknown narrator
    c. Third person point of view limited to Alice's perspective
    d. Third person point of view with multiple characters' perspectives
    e. Second person point of view from the perspective of Alice

27. What might the rabbit hole symbolize in the story?
    a. The rabbit hole represents Alice's childhood.
    b. The rabbit hole represents the unknown of adulthood and what the future holds.
    c. The rabbit hole is a symbol of Alice's willingness to try new things.
    d. The rabbit hole acts as a symbol of reality in this fantasy world.
    e. The rabbit hole represents Alice's lack of inhibition.

28. What do the lines, "'How funny it'll seem to come out among the people that walk with their heads downward! The Antipathies, I think—' (she was rather glad there was no one listening, this time, as it didn't sound at all the right word) '—but I shall have to ask them what the name of the country is, you know'" reveal about Alice's character?
    a. Alice is not very intelligent.
    b. Alice is very curious.
    c. Alice does not understand what is happening to her.
    d. Alice has lost her mind.
    e. Alice is concerned with what others think of her.

29. When the white rabbit says, "Oh my ears and whiskers, how late it's getting!" it is an example of which of the following?
    a. Imagery
    b. Symbolism
    c. Foreshadowing
    d. Exposition
    e. Characterization

30. What is Alice's state of mind at the end of the passage?
    a. She is curious about where the rabbit is going.
    b. She is eager to find out what will happen next.
    c. She is regretful and worried that she may not be able to get out.
    d. She is worried that the rabbit will not come back to help her.
    e. She is worried that her sister will come down after her.

Questions 31 through 40 refer to the following passage:

Knowing that Mrs. Mallard was afflicted with a heart trouble, great care was taken to break to her as gently as possible the news of her husband's death.

It was her sister Josephine who told her, in broken sentences; veiled hints that revealed in half concealing. Her husband's friend Richards was there, too, near her. It was he who had been in the newspaper office when intelligence of the railroad disaster was received, with Brently Mallard's name leading the list of "killed." He had only taken the time to assure himself of its truth by a second telegram, and had hastened to forestall any less careful, less tender friend in bearing the sad message.

She did not hear the story as many women have heard the same, with a paralyzed inability to accept its significance. She wept at once, with sudden, wild abandonment, in her sister's arms. When the storm of grief had spent itself she went away to her room alone. She would have no one follow her.

There stood, facing the open window, a comfortable, roomy armchair. Into this she sank, pressed down by a physical exhaustion that haunted her body and seemed to reach into her soul.

She could see in the open square before her house the tops of trees that were all aquiver with the new spring life. The delicious breath of rain was in the air. In the street below a peddler was crying his wares. The notes of a distant song, which some one was singing reached her faintly, and countless sparrows were twittering in the eaves.

There were patches of blue sky showing here and there through the clouds that had met and piled one above the other in the west facing her window.

She sat with her head thrown back upon the cushion of the chair, quite motionless, except when a sob came up into her throat and shook her, as a child who has cried itself to sleep continues to sob in its dreams.

She was young, with a fair, calm face, whose lines bespoke repression and even a certain strength. But now there was a dull stare in her eyes, whose gaze was fixed away off yonder on one of those patches of blue sky. It was not a glance of reflection, but rather indicated a suspension of intelligent thought.

There was something coming to her and she was waiting for it, fearfully. What was it? She did not know; it was too subtle and elusive to name. But she felt it, creeping out of the sky, reaching toward her through the sounds, the scents, the color that filled the air.

Now her bosom rose and fell tumultuously. She was beginning to recognize this thing that was approaching to possess her, and she was striving to beat it back with her will—as powerless as her two white slender hands would have been. When she abandoned herself a little whispered word escaped her slightly parted lips. She said it over and over under her breath: "free, free, free!" The vacant stare and the look of terror that had followed it went from her eyes. They stayed keen and bright. Her pulses beat fast, and the coursing blood warmed and relaxed every inch of her body.

She did not stop to ask if it were or were not a monstrous joy that held her. A clear and exalted perception enabled her to dismiss the suggestion as trivial. She knew that she would weep again when she saw the kind, tender hands folded in death; the face that had never looked save with love upon her, fixed and gray and dead. But she saw beyond that bitter moment a long procession of years to come that would belong to her absolutely. And she opened and spread her arms out to them in welcome.

There would be no one to live for during those coming years; she would live for herself. There would be no powerful will bending hers in that blind persistence with which men and women believe they have a right to impose a private will upon a fellow-creature. A kind intention or a cruel intention made the act seem no less a crime as she looked upon it in that brief moment of illumination.

And yet she had loved him--sometimes. Often she had not. What did it matter! What could love, the unsolved mystery, count for in the face of this possession of self-assertion which she suddenly recognized as the strongest impulse of her being!

"Free! Body and soul free!" she kept whispering.

Josephine was kneeling before the closed door with her lips to the keyhole, imploring for admission. "Louise, open the door! I beg; open the door—you will make yourself ill. What are you doing, Louise? For heaven's sake open the door."

"Go away. I am not making myself ill." No; she was drinking in a very elixir of life through that open window.

Her fancy was running riot along those days ahead of her. Spring days, and summer days, and all sorts of days that would be her own. She breathed a quick prayer that life might be long. It was only yesterday she had thought with a shudder that life might be long.

She arose at length and opened the door to her sister's importunities. There was a feverish triumph in her eyes, and she carried herself unwittingly like a goddess of Victory. She clasped her sister's waist, and together they descended the stairs. Richards stood waiting for them at the bottom.

Some one was opening the front door with a latchkey. It was Brently Mallard who entered, a little travel-stained, composedly carrying his grip-sack and umbrella. He had been far from the scene of the accident, and did not even know there had been one. He stood amazed at Josephine's piercing cry; at Richards' quick motion to screen him from the view of his wife.

When the doctors came they said she had died of heart disease—of the joy that kills.

"The Story of an Hour" by Kate Chopin (1894)

31. An important symbol in the story is identified in which of the following lines?
    a. "He stood amazed at Josephine's piercing cry; at Richards' quick motion to screen him from the view of his wife."
    b. "She could see in the open square before her house the tops of trees that were all aquiver with the new spring life."
    c. "It was her sister Josephine who told her, in broken sentences; veiled hints that revealed in half concealing."
    d. "Her pulses beat fast, and the coursing blood warmed and relaxed every inch of her body."
    e. "There was something coming to her and she was waiting for it, fearfully."

32. What is the meaning of the word *importunities* in the passage?
    a. Urgent or persistent solicitation
    b. Occurring at an inconvenient time
    c. A set of circumstances that make it possible to do something
    d. An important message
    e. Not desirable or optimistic

33. When the doctors say that Mrs. Mallard "died of heart disease—of the joy that kills," it can be inferred that:
    a. She died from a heart attack.
    b. Her heart was defective.
    c. She died because of the joy she experienced seeing her husband alive.
    d. She died because of the joy she felt at potentially being free of her marriage.
    e. Mr. Mallard was responsible for her death.

34. What do the lines, "She did not stop to ask if it were or were not a monstrous joy that held her. A clear and exalted perception enabled her to dismiss the suggestion as trivial," say about Mrs. Mallard's state of mind?
    a. She is not concerned with the fact that she is happy, even though she has just been given the news that her husband is dead.
    b. She is confused about how she feels now that she knows her husband is dead.
    c. She is extremely happy that her husband is dead.
    d. She feels like a monster because she is not sad that her husband is dead.
    e. She believes her husband was a monster and deserved to die, so she is happy.

35. What does this story suggest about Kate Chopin's feelings on marriage?
    a. Women should choose a kind man to marry in order to realize happiness.
    b. Bad marriages should be ended by any means possible, even death.
    c. Women shouldn't marry oppressive men like Mr. Mallard.
    d. Mrs. Mallard should have divorced Mr. Mallard.
    e. Marriage, even in its best form, is oppressive to women.

36. The "blue sky," referred to several times throughout the story, is an example of which of the following?
    a. Personification
    b. Imagery
    c. Theme
    d. Setting
    e. Point of view

37. From which point of view is "The Story of an Hour" told?
    a. First person point of view from Mrs. Mallard's perspective
    b. First person point of view from Josephine's perspective
    c. Third person point of view limited to Josephine's perspective
    d. Third person point of view limited to Mrs. Mallard's perspective
    e. Third person point of view from both Josephine's and Mrs. Mallard's perspective

38. Which of the following can be assumed from the line, "What could love, the unsolved mystery, count for in the face of this possession of self-assertion which she suddenly recognized as the strongest impulse of her being!"?
    a. Mrs. Mallard never loved Mr. Mallard.
    b. Mrs. Mallard believes that her freedom is worth more than love.
    c. Mrs. Mallard doesn't believe in love.
    d. Mrs. Mallard is devastated that the love of her life is dead.
    e. Mrs. Mallard is fearful of her new reality.

39. Which of the following best describes the change in the outlook of Mrs. Mallard once she is told Mr. Mallard is dead?
    a. Fearful to elated
    b. Weak to strong
    c. Regretful to fearful
    d. Powerful to powerless
    e. Devastated to content

40. Based on the line, "He had only taken the time to assure himself of its truth by a second telegram, and had hastened to forestall any less careful, less tender friend in bearing the sad message," which of the following can be assumed?
  a. Richards wants to be absolutely positive that Mr. Mallard is dead.
  b. Richards is afraid to tell Mrs. Mallard of his death because of her heart condition.
  c. Richards wants to tell Mrs. Mallard of his death before someone else does.
  d. Richards hopes someone else will deliver the news to Mrs. Mallard so he doesn't have to.
  e. Richards receives conflicting telegrams of Mr. Mallard's death.

Questions 41 through 50 refer to the following passage:

Let America be America again.

Let it be the dream it used to be.

Let it be the pioneer on the plain

Seeking a home where he himself is free.

(America never was America to me.)

Let America be the dream the dreamers dreamed—

Let it be that great strong land of love

Where never kings connive nor tyrants scheme

That any man be crushed by one above.

(It never was America to me.)

O, let my land be a land where Liberty

Is crowned with no false patriotic wreath,

But opportunity is real, and life is free,

Equality is in the air we breathe.

(There's never been equality for me,

Nor freedom in this "homeland of the free.")

Say, who are you that mumbles in the dark?

And who are you that draws your veil across the stars?

I am the poor white, fooled and pushed apart,

I am the Negro bearing slavery's scars.

I am the red man driven from the land,

I am the immigrant clutching the hope I seek—

And finding only the same old stupid plan

Of dog eat dog, of mighty crush the weak.

I am the young man, full of strength and hope,

Tangled in that ancient endless chain

Of profit, power, gain, of grab the land!

Of grab the gold! Of grab the ways of satisfying need!

Of work the men! Of take the pay!

Of owning everything for one's own greed!

I am the farmer, bondsman to the soil.

I am the worker sold to the machine.

I am the Negro, servant to you all.

I am the people, humble, hungry, mean—

Hungry yet today despite the dream.

Beaten yet today—O, Pioneers!

I am the man who never got ahead,

The poorest worker bartered through the years.

Yet I'm the one who dreamt our basic dream

In the Old World while still a serf of kings,

Who dreamt a dream so strong, so brave, so true,

That even yet its mighty daring sings

In every brick and stone, in every furrow turned

That's made America the land it has become.

O, I'm the man who sailed those early seas

In search of what I meant to be my home—

For I'm the one who left dark Ireland's shore,

And Poland's plain, and England's grassy lea,

And torn from Black Africa's strand I came

To build a "homeland of the free."

The free?

Who said the free? Not me?

Surely not me? The millions on relief today?

The millions shot down when we strike?

The millions who have nothing for our pay?

For all the dreams we've dreamed

And all the songs we've sung

And all the hopes we've held

And all the flags we've hung,

The millions who have nothing for our pay—

Except the dream that's almost dead today.

O, let America be America again—

The land that never has been yet—

And yet must be—the land where *every* man is free.

The land that's mine—the poor man's, Indian's, Negro's, ME—

Who made America,

Whose sweat and blood, whose faith and pain,

Whose hand at the foundry, whose plow in the rain,

Must bring back our mighty dream again.

Sure, call me any ugly name you choose—

The steel of freedom does not stain.

From those who live like leeches on the people's lives,

We must take back our land again,

America!

O, yes,

I say it plain,

America never was America to me,

And yet I swear this oath—

America will be!

Out of the rack and ruin of our gangster death,

The rape and rot of graft, and stealth, and lies,

We, the people, must redeem

The land, the mines, the plants, the rivers.

The mountains and the endless plain—

All, all the stretch of these great green states—

And make America again!

"Let America Be America Again" by Langston Hughes'

Questions 41 through 50 refer to the following passage:

41. Which literary device is exemplified in the line, "Let it be the pioneer on the plain"?
    a. Alliteration
    b. Imagery
    c. Personification
    d. Rhyme scheme
    e. Foreshadowing

42. What is the central focus of the poem?
    a. Slavery
    b. Freedom
    c. Pioneers
    d. Immigration
    e. The American Dream

43. In the stanza that begins "Who said the free?" which answer best describes the theme?
    a. The American Dream is possible for everyone.
    b. Freedom is only attainable in America.
    c. The American Dream is dead.
    d. Inequality has made the American Dream nearly impossible for some.
    e. No one understands the American Dream better than the poor.

44. What is the point of view of the poem?
    a. Third person limited point of view
    b. Third person objective point of view
    c. First person point of view
    d. Second person point of view
    e. Third person omniscient point of view

45. What do the lines, "I am the poor white, fooled and pushed apart, / I am the Negro bearing slavery's scars. / I am the red man driven from the land, / I am the immigrant clutching the hope I seek—," suggest about the speaker?
    a. He is speaking for all Americans.
    b. The speaker is multiracial.
    c. The poem is being told by an unknown narrator.
    d. The speaker is Native American.
    e. The speaker is a slave.

46. What is the speaker's tone in the lines, "O, let America be America again—/ The land that never has been yet— / And yet must be—the land where *every* man is free. / The land that's mine—the poor man's, Indian's, Negro's, ME—"?
    a. Hopeful
    b. Joyful
    c. Melancholy
    d. Ironic
    e. Excited

47. What does "its" refer to in the lines, "That even yet its mighty daring sings, / In every brick and stone, in every furrow turned"?
  a. The Old World
  b. Americans
  c. The American Dream
  d. The king
  e. The serfs

48. What is the central idea in the lines, "Out of the rack and ruin of our gangster death, / The rape and rot of graft, and stealth, and lies, / We, the people, must redeem / The land, the mines, the plants, the rivers."?
  a. People must rise up from what America has become and reclaim their land.
  b. America has been irreparably ruined by crime.
  c. Americans have destroyed the land.
  d. Secrets and lies will be the ruin of America.
  e. America cannot overcome its terrible past.

49. In the line, "the dream the dreamers dreamed," which literary device is used?
  a. Imagery
  b. Symbolism
  c. Metaphor
  d. Alliteration
  e. Personification

50. The repetition of this sentiment in the lines "(It never was America to me.)" and "(America never was America to me.)" suggests which of the following about Hughes' theme?
  a. He feels left out of the American Dream.
  b. He admonishes America for what it has become.
  c. America is not the land of the free.
  d. He does not want to live in America anymore.
  e. He doesn't live in America.

Questions 51 through 60 refer to the following passage:

North Richmond Street, being blind, was a quiet street except at the hour when the Christian Brothers' School set the boys free. An uninhabited house of two storeys stood at the blind end, detached from its neighbours in a square ground. The other houses of the street, conscious of decent lives within them, gazed at one another with brown imperturbable faces.

The former tenant of our house, a priest, had died in the back drawing-room. Air, musty from having been long enclosed, hung in all the rooms, and the waste room behind the kitchen was littered with old useless papers. Among these I found a few paper-covered books, the pages of which were curled and damp: The Abbot, by Walter Scott, The Devout Communicant, and The Memoirs of Vidocq. I liked the last best because its leaves were yellow. The wild garden behind the house contained a central apple-tree and a few straggling bushes, under one of which I found the late tenant's rusty bicycle-pump. He had been a very charitable priest; in his will he had left all his money to institutions and the furniture of his house to his sister.

When the short days of winter came, dusk fell before we had well eaten our dinners. When we met in the street the houses had grown sombre. The space of sky above us was the colour of ever-changing violet and towards it the lamps of the street lifted their feeble lanterns. The cold air stung us and we played till our bodies glowed. Our shouts echoed in the silent street. The career of our play brought us through the dark muddy lanes behind the houses, where we ran the gauntlet of the rough tribes from the cottages, to the back doors of the dark dripping gardens where odours arose from the ashpits, to the dark odorous stables where a coachman smoothed and combed the horse or shook music from the buckled harness. When we returned to the street, light from the kitchen windows had filled the areas. If my uncle was seen turning the corner, we hid in the shadow until we had seen him safely housed. Or if Mangan's sister came out on the doorstep to call her brother in to his tea, we watched her from our shadow peer up and down the street. We waited to see whether she would remain or go in and, if she remained, we left our shadow and walked up to Mangan's steps resignedly. She was waiting for us, her figure defined by the light from the half-opened door. Her brother always teased her before he obeyed, and I stood by the railings looking at her. Her dress swung as she moved her body, and the soft rope of her hair tossed from side to side.

Every morning I lay on the floor in the front parlour watching her door. The blind was pulled down to within an inch of the sash so that I could not be seen. When she came out on the doorstep my heart leaped. I ran to the hall, seized my books and followed her. I kept her brown figure always in my eye and, when we came near the point at which our ways diverged, I quickened my pace and passed her. This happened morning after morning. I had never spoken to her, except for a few casual words, and yet her name was like a summons to all my foolish blood.

Her image accompanied me even in places the most hostile to romance. On Saturday evenings when my aunt went marketing I had to go to carry some of the parcels. We walked through the flaring streets, jostled by drunken men and bargaining women, amid the curses of labourers, the shrill litanies of shop-boys who stood on guard by the barrels of pigs' cheeks, the nasal chanting of street-singers, who sang a come-all-you about O'Donovan Rossa, or a ballad about the troubles in our native land. These noises converged in a single sensation of life for me: I imagined that I bore my chalice safely through a throng of foes. Her name sprang to my lips at moments in strange prayers and praises which I myself did not understand. My eyes were often full of tears (I could not tell why) and at times a flood from my heart seemed to pour itself out into my bosom. I thought little of the future. I did not know whether I would ever speak to her or not or, if I spoke to her, how I could tell her of my confused adoration. But my body was like a harp and her words and gestures were like fingers running upon the wires.

"Araby" by James Joyce (1914)

51. The opening paragraph of the story includes an example of which of the following?
    a. Simile
    b. Personification
    c. Symbolism
    d. Theme
    e. Characterization

52. Who is narrating the story?
    a. Araby
    b. An unknown narrator
    c. Mangan
    d. Mangan's sister
    e. A lovesick schoolboy

53. What is the meaning of the word *imperturbable* in the first paragraph?
    a. Repulsive
    b. Unconcerned
    c. Unadorned
    d. Ornate
    e. Monotonous

54. In the lines, "This happened morning after morning. I had never spoken to her, except for a few casual words, and yet her name was like a summons to all my foolish blood," which of the following can be inferred about the narrator?
    a. He feels foolish because he's afraid to speak to her.
    b. He is afraid Mangan will find out that he has feelings for his sister.
    c. He is afraid of Mangan's sister.
    d. He is drawn to Mangan's sister even though he's barely spoken to her.
    e. He is unaware of how much Mangan's sister has feelings for him as well.

55. The line, "to the back doors of the dark dripping gardens where odours arose from the ashpits, to the dark odorous stables where a coachman smoothed and combed the horse or shook music from the buckled harness," is an example of which of the following?
    a. Imagery
    b. Theme
    c. Personification
    d. Characterization
    e. Symbolism

56. What is the narrator's state of mind in the final paragraph of the passage?
    a. Pining
    b. Bewildered
    c. Amused
    d. Desperate
    e. Disconcerted

57. What purpose does the third paragraph of the passage serve?
    a. To describe the state of mind of the narrator
    b. To provide exposition of the setting
    c. To symbolize the innocence of childhood
    d. To introduce new characters, the neighborhood boys
    e. To express Joyce's theme about the importance of friendship

58. Based on the passage, it can be inferred that Joyce's central theme is which of the following?
    a. Boys will be boys.
    b. Love is wasted on the young.
    c. The transition from boyhood to manhood is a confusing time.
    d. Friendship is more important than love.
    e. Boys experience love differently than girls.

59. Which of the following best describes the point of view of "Araby"?
    a. First person with a narrator telling memories of his youth
    b. Third person with a narrator telling the story of the boy
    c. Third person with a narrator telling his own story
    d. First person with an unknown narrator telling the story
    e. Second person with a narrator telling his own story

60. What might be the reason for including the description of the former tenant in the second paragraph?
    a. Exposing background on the main character and his living conditions
    b. Foreshadowing the importance of religion in his life
    c. Showing that his parents are very religious
    d. Creating a mood of sadness since the tenant died
    e. Providing characterization of the priest, an important character in the story

Answer Explanations

1. D: In this passage, Juliet says, "that which we call a rose By any other name would smell as sweet," meaning that regardless of Romeo's name, he is still Romeo. She would still love him and see him as perfection, no matter his title. She isn't saying that she is special here or that Romeo shouldn't love her. While the titles of Capulet and Montague are what keep them apart, she is not saying that here. Her main point is that their names are meaningless when it comes to their love.

2. B: The sun is rising and shining, but that is not why the moon is envious. Romeo is comparing Juliet's beauty to the sun. He is essentially saying that the moon pales in comparison to Juliet's beauty and should be envious of how she shines. He says the moon is sick with grief because Juliet is so much more beautiful. While the moon is paler than the sun, this doesn't best describe Romeo's intention with this statement.

3. A: Romeo has seen Juliet and is desperate to be with her. Lines like "it is my love O that she knew she were" and "That I might touch that cheek!" indicate that he desires to touch and be with Juliet. He does not demonstrate any sadness or remorsefulness in these lines. While he may respect Juliet, he is more enamored with her than respectful in his tone. He is neither tentative nor hesitant, as he is describing her beauty with desire and love.

4. C: Romeo compares Juliet to a winged messenger of heaven because he hears her voice over his head. This, along with the set direction, suggests that she is above him on the balcony, and he is in the garden. The other lines do not suggest anything about Romeo's proximity to Juliet in the play.

5. B: Romeo uses the word *as* to compare Juliet to the winged messenger of heaven. This comparison using *like* or *as* is a simile. An example of a metaphor would be "Juliet is the sun" because it does not use the words *like* or *as*. An example of personification would be when Romeo describes the moon as envious. Imagery and theme are not demonstrated in this example.

6. E: Imagery refers to anything that appeals to the senses, such as birds singing. In all the other examples, there are no appeals to the senses. The birds singing is an example of an auditory image, appealing to the sense of hearing.

7. D: In this line, the sun is personified. It is given the human characteristic of being able to kill the moon, which is also personified here. None of the other lines give human qualities to something that is not human.

8. C: In this passage, Shakespeare shows Romeo's and Juliet's love for one another. Romeo sees Juliet as the sun, and Juliet denounces her name for him. This shows the power of their young love. While they may seem foolish, Shakespeare takes this more seriously than that and does not denounce them for their feelings. In the end, they are parted through death. While Romeo compares Juliet to things found in nature, he does not say she is more beautiful than the sun, but that she is the sun. Nature is not indicated to be more important than love here.

9. A: Juliet doesn't actually say anything here. What Romeo means is that her beauty speaks for her. Romeo is looking at her from afar and couldn't hear her even if she did speak. He mentions her eyes, but not that she looks at him. She doesn't know that he is there at this point.

10. A: Juliet states, "And for that name which is no part of thee Take all myself," which means she wants Romeo to trade his name for her. She likely wants to marry Romeo, which would mean to leave her family, but this is a more powerful statement than that. She is offering her whole self if he will renounce his name.

11. C: In this poem, the speaker is an unnamed narrator. Though the poem does mention a man and discusses how he might enjoy the solitude of working on a farm, he is used as part of an analogy, not the speaker of the poem. There is no mention of a young girl in the poem or any references that would indicate she is the speaker.

12. A: In this poem, the speaker is reflecting on the joys of solitude. The poet's tone is pensive, as he considers the peace that being alone can offer. Dejected and despondent are not the correct tone, as they both mean sad or depressed. *Indignant* is a synonym for angry, which is not appropriate here. While the poet does express joy in solitude, it is more in a sense of satisfaction than the sense of excitement the word *buoyant* indicates.

13. C: The line "A few paternal acres bound" suggests that the man owns land that was passed down from his father. The word *paternal* means "of or appropriate to a father." Paternal is used to describe the land, not the man. It does not indicate that he works for his father or that his father is still living. Subsequent lines state that he owns the land. Paternal does not suggest that the land is made up of pastures.

14. E: The speaker is asking to live "unknown" and "unseen" in his solitude. He also wishes to die in the same manner. He asks for his death to be "unlamented," as he is content with his solitary life and feels the same about his death. This does not indicate that he is lonely, and he has not lost his will to live. Nothing in the poem suggests that he is ill or wants to die. This stanza instead refers to the manner in which he wishes to both live and die, which is in solitude.

15. D: These lines suggest that his crops provide him with food, in this case the grain to grow bread. The herds produce milk for him to drink, and the sheep provide wool for clothes. The overall impression is that the farm provides him with everything he needs for his solitary life. While the farm is productive and he is likely busy on the farm, the overall impression is that the farm meets all of his needs.

16. A: This is an ode, which is a lyric poem addressed to the subject of solitude. A song narrating a story is a ballad. A lengthy narrative poem dealing with heroic deeds is an epic. A poem of serious reflection, lamenting the dead, is an elegy. A work dealing with rural life and its contrast to city life is a pastoral poem. While this has pastoral elements and does mention death, it is above all an ode.

17. E: The farm where the man lives is where the poem is set. Imagery relates to the senses, theme is the poet's message, character is the man, and symbolism refers to objects that repeat.

18. C: The man realizes in the end that he would like to die "unlamented," or without fanfare. His simple life of solitude was peaceful and satisfying, and he would like his death to be the same. He is not lonely, but content with his life on the farm. Though his farm was successful to him, this is not the realization he comes to in the end. There is no indication that he is regretful or will miss his life when he dies.

19. A: The definition of the word *unlamented* is to not mourn or regret a person who has died. Regret would be the opposite of unlamented. Alone, inconsolable, and not loved do not accurately define unlamented.

20. B: Theme is the poet's message about the subject matter. In the fourth stanza, he states, "study and ease, / Together mixed; sweet recreation; / And innocence, which most does please," which suggests that happiness can be found in the balance of both work (study) and play (recreation). This is not an example of imagery, symbolism, setting, or character.

21. B: Alice is described as tired of watching her sister read, and considering other activities such as making a daisy chain. The hot weather has made her sleepy and stupid. All of this indicates that she is weary or bored. Her mood has not quite reached irritable, and she is not insolent or rude. She is looking for ways to amuse herself but does not appear to be amused yet. *Indignant* means to show anger, and Alice does not appear to be angry here.

22. D: When Carroll gives background information about characters and setting, he is demonstrating exposition. A euphemism is a polite expression used to describe something unpleasant, which is not present here. Imagery is language that appeals to the senses. While there is imagery in the passage, revealing the background information is not considered imagery. Personification, or giving human qualities to objects, is not used here. Metaphor, or comparisons without the use of *like* or **as,** are also not used here.

23. C: *Alice's Adventures in Wonderland* is classified as a fantasy novel, meaning it is set in an alternate world, which may contain unrealistic elements. In the real world, Alice's fall would be very quick, and she would likely not have time to think or do anything but scream. In the fantasy world that Carroll has created, Alice has time to consider her fall in detail, see cupboards and maps, and take down a jar of marmalade from a shelf. This reveals to the audience that the work is not rooted in reality and is indeed a fantasy novel. While the fall may be mysterious and even scary, this is not a mystery or horror novel. Nothing indicates that the novel is romantic in nature.

24. B: Alice is an overwhelmingly curious character. She sees the rabbit and immediately follows him down the hole without thinking of how she will get out, because she is curious, not unintelligent. Her intelligence is revealed as she carefully considers what she is seeing during her long fall. While she is described as bored at the start of the passage, this action is a result of her curiosity more than anything. The act isn't necessarily brave or courageous, and it does not reveal her to be insane, as it's only natural for a person to be curious about a rabbit in a waistcoat.

25. A: In this line, Alice considers what her actions and this experience will do to others' perceptions of her. This reveals her considering her identity and how she fits into the world. The other lines do not exemplify Alice pondering her identity or her place in the world.

26. C: The story is told in third person limited point of view. The reader is given only Alice's perspective through an unknown narrator. Readers do not have access to any other character's thoughts or feelings. It is not written in first or second point of view due to the absence of personal pronouns like *I, me, we, us, you,* and *your*.

27. B: Ultimately, *Alice's Adventures in Wonderland* is about the loss of innocence. Going down the rabbit hole represents Alice taking a step into adulthood and the future. The rabbit hole represents the unknown, not Alice's childhood or her willingness to try new things or lack of inhibition. It is more a representation of the fantasy world than reality.

28. E: These lines mostly reveal that Alice, though she is falling down a well, is more concerned with what people might think if they heard of her lack of knowledge. She is a child, so this doesn't reveal a lack of knowledge or understanding; rather it reveals that she is very concerned with knowing the right words. She is not crazy, though she talks to herself. This is done for effect to illustrate her state of mind.

29. C: The rabbit regularly references time and that it is running out. The clock is running out on Alice's childhood. These words foreshadow what is about to happen in Alice's life. This line is not an example of imagery or symbolism, as no sensory images or symbolic objects are identified. It does not necessarily expose any information about characters or setting.

30. C: Alice does not see a way out and is realizing that she probably shouldn't have come down after the rabbit. Her curiosity has dissipated, and she is now worried that her impulsiveness has gotten the better of her. She is not necessarily eager to follow the rabbit or for him to come back. There is no indication that she is concerned her sister will follow her down the rabbit hole. She is more concerned with herself and her own way out.

31. B: In this line, the "open square" refers to the window Mrs. Mallard looks out in her room. None of the other sentences identify a symbol, which is an object that repeats and/or has significant meaning in the story. The window symbolizes her new view of the world, now that she believes she is free of her marriage.

32. A: The definition of *importunities* as it is used in the passage is urgent, persistent solicitation. Josephine is at the door begging Mrs. Mallard repeatedly to open the door. The other answers do not adequately define importunities.

33. D: Mrs. Mallard is overjoyed that she may have a chance at life without the confines of her marriage. This is the joy that kills her. She may have heart trouble, but that can be taken figuratively in that she is unhappy in her marriage. Mrs. Mallard wishes to be free of her husband, so she is not overjoyed that he has come home alive. Nothing in the passage indicates that Mr. Mallard is responsible for Mrs. Mallard's death.

34. A: Mrs. Mallard does not stop to consider that the joy she feels may be inappropriate in the wake of her husband's death. She is too overcome with this new feeling of freedom to care. She is not confused about her feelings anymore, as she recognizes this new feeling as joy in her new situation. Though the lines indicate that the joy she feels might be inappropriate, she does not feel like a monster. Nothing in the lines indicate that Mr. Mallard is a bad man or deserved to die, just that Mrs. Mallard is happy to be free of her marriage.

35. E: The story reveals that Mr. Mallard is kind to Mrs. Mallard, and indeed she is terrified at first at the idea of being free of her marriage. She eventually realizes that even though Mr. Mallard is a fine man, she wants to be free from him and the confines of marriage. Chopin does not suggest that women need to be in a good marriage. The fact that Mr. Mallard is kind shows that it is marriage, not the man a woman marries, that is oppressive. She does not suggest that women shouldn't marry a particular man or that Mrs. Mallard should have ended the marriage by any means necessary, but that the institution of marriage is inherently oppressive to women.

36. B: The blue sky is a sensory image representing Mrs. Mallard's glimpse into her future. Chopin does not use personification when referring to the blue sky. The blue sky is not used as a theme in the story. The setting is Mrs. Mallard's house and, more specifically, her room, not the blue sky. The blue sky is not an example of point of view, which is the perspective from which the story is told.

37. D: The story is told in third person limited point of view. An unknown narrator shares the perspective of Mrs. Mallard. While Josephine is an important character in the story, readers only get to see what she does and hear what she says. They do not have access to her inner thoughts or her perspective on the story. The story does not use first person point of view.

38. B: In this passage, Mrs. Mallard is saying that in the face of her potential freedom from the confines of marriage, love is meaningless. She realizes that she wants her freedom with all of her heart, regardless of whether or not she loved her husband. She does say that she loved him sometimes, and that shows that she believes in love, but that it doesn't compare to her freedom. She is upset that Mr. Mallard is dead, but she is more overwhelmed by the feelings of joy she is experiencing now that she is free. At first, she is fearful of this new reality, but in this passage, she recognizes that this is exactly what she wants with all her being.

39. A: When Mrs. Mallard is first told that her husband is dead, she is fearful of her new position and what it means. As she recognizes the feeling as joy that she is free, she is elated. Mrs. Mallard is generally described as weak of heart at the start of the story, but the emotion seen once she is told of Mr. Mallard's apparent death is fear, not weakness. Mrs. Mallard expresses her regret that Mr. Mallard has passed, but her regret turns to joy, not fear. If anything, Mrs. Mallard goes from powerless to powerful when she realizes she is free. She is upset that Mr. Mallard is gone, but not devastated, and her feeling turns to elation, not content.

40. C: Richards receives two telegrams confirming Mr. Mallard's death and hurries to share the news with Mrs. Mallard before someone else delivers the news in a less delicate way than he could. He considers this enough notice that the news is true, and though he may be concerned about telling Mrs. Mallard, that is not the main impression to be taken from these lines. He hopes to be the first to tell her, and nothing here suggests the telegrams are conflicting.

41. C: In this line, *it* refers to America, and it is being personified as a pioneer. There is no alliteration in the line. Imagery refers to the senses, and there is no reference to that here. The stanza contains a rhyme scheme, but this particular line does not. This line does not appear to foreshadow anything else in the poem.

42. E: Langston Hughes' major focus in this poem is the American Dream. The speaker repeatedly comes back to this dream and what it means to him. While he does mention slavery, it is only part of the poem, and not the central focus. He briefly mentions pioneers in the first stanza, but again, this is not the overall focus of the poem. Immigration is implied, but it is also not the main focus of the poem.

43. D: The lines in this stanza suggest that those who are on government assistance, those who are struck down when protesting, the underpaid, are not free. The dream is nearly dead for them because they are not treated equally, so it is not possible for everyone. These lines do not suggest anything about freedom solely in America. Hughes says that the dream is nearly dead, but not dead entirely. While he does mention those who are underpaid, he is not saying they are the only ones who understand the American Dream.

44. C: The poem uses first person point of view from the perspective of an unknown speaker. He does identify himself as many different characters, but only to make the point that he is speaking for all Americans in this poem. The other points of view are incorrect.

45. A: The speaker suggests that he is white, black, and Native American to make the point that he is speaking for Americans of every race. He is not one person, but many people who have been treated unfairly in some way and denied the American Dream. The speaker is not necessarily multiracial, Native American, or a slave, as this is being used as a metaphor. The speaker of the poem is not unknown. The reader is provided some details about who the speaker is.

46. A: The use of the words *O* and *let* suggest that the speaker is wishful that things could be different. He hopes for America to be a place where everyone is free. The italics on the word *every* suggest that he is more hopeful than joyful here. He wants something that he hasn't experienced. He says this in a way that is hopeful rather than sad or ironic. He is not necessarily excited in these lines.

47. C: *Its* refers to the dream the speaker dreamed of in the Old World. It is the hope for a better life that the American Dream promises. He mentions the Old World, kings, and serfs in the preceding lines, but only in his description of the American Dream. *Its* does not refer to Americans as a whole, but the dream for America.

48. A: These lines suggest that Americans must rise up from the crime, secrets, and lies of the past and reclaim the land and the American Dream. It calls for people to leave the terrible past behind. The lines do not suggest that the damage is irreparable or that the land is destroyed. While secrets and lies may be to blame, he does not indicate that America is ruined or cannot be redeemed. Hughes suggests much the opposite. He is calling for Americans to take back what is theirs and overcome the mistakes of the past.

49. D: The repetitive use of the same consonant sound at the start of each word is an example of alliteration. This is not an example of imagery, symbolism, metaphor, or personification.

50. A: These particular parenthetical statements are powerful interjections in the poem. They show that he feels left out of the American Dream, as if it doesn't apply to him and others like him. While he does admonish America and state that some people are not free in the poem, these particular lines are more about his own identity and place in America. These lines and the poem in general do not suggest that he doesn't want to live in America or that he is not American.

51. B: In the opening line, the narrator gives human qualities to the houses gazing at one another. This paragraph does not include a comparison using *like* or *as*, or simile. It does not contain any clear symbols. It does not include the author's message, or theme. It does not introduce any characters in detail beyond the generic mention of "boys."

52. E: The story is told in first person point of view from the perspective of a character in the story, who mentions school books and his crush on a neighbor. While he is unnamed, he is not unknown. "Araby" is the title of the story and is not mentioned in the passage. Mangan is a friend of the narrator, and his sister is the object of the narrator's affections.

53. B: The correct meaning of the word *unperturbed* is unconcerned. In this case, Joyce personifies the houses, saying they are unconcerned with what is going on around them, or unperturbed. The other answers do not correctly define unperturbed.

54. D: The narrator is young and just discovering feelings for a woman for the first time. He feels inexplicably drawn to her and aroused by the mere sound of her name. He does not feel foolish for being afraid to speak to her, nor does he suggest that he is fearful here. Instead, he is more a fool for love. There is no indication in these lines that Mangan's sister has feelings for the narrator.

55. A: This line describes the smells of the ashpits, the stables, and the musical sounds of the horses, all of which are sensory images. Theme is the author's message about the subject, which is not seen here. Nothing is personified, and no characterization is present. While there are objects mentioned, it is in the context of imagery, not symbolism.

56. A: In the final paragraph, Mangan's sister has taken over the narrator's mind. He is consumed with her and is pining for her. He is confused earlier in the passage, but at this point he is beginning to understand his feelings and the power they have over him. He is not amused or desperate, and nothing in the passage suggests he is disconcerted. Instead, he is filled with lust for Mangan's sister, and so *pining* is the best word to describe his state of mind.

57. B: This passage mainly describes the narrator's surroundings. It includes descriptive language of the neighborhood and indicates the time of life and time in history when the story may have taken place. The character's state of mind takes a back seat to the setting in this paragraph. There are some elements of the innocence of childhood, but no real symbols that are significant or that repeat. The neighborhood boys are briefly mentioned, but not fully described. While Joyce may feel friendship is important, this paragraph is more about exposing the setting than delivering a message about friendship.

58. C: At this point in the passage, it is clear that this is a coming-of-age tale. James Joyce's message is that this time, the transition from boyhood to manhood, is confusing. The character goes back and forth from playing with his childhood friends to obsessing over his love interest and his awakening sexuality.

59. A: "Araby" is told in first person point of view. The narrator is a character in the story, and he is writing from memory of his youth. The story is not told in third or second person, as evidenced by the use of personal pronouns (*I, me, we, us*). The narrator is not unknown, as many details are provided about him and his life.

60. A: Including the description of the tenant and his living quarters reveals some details about the narrator and the way he lives. Religion is important in his life, but this paragraph is used to expose setting and character more than the importance of religion. The boy's parents are not mentioned in the passage. The fact that the tenant died is delivered as a matter of fact, without much sadness or regret. The priest is not revealed to be an important character in the story.

Dear SAT Literature Test Taker,

We would like to start by thanking you for purchasing this study guide for your SAT Literature exam. We hope that we exceeded your expectations.

Our goal in creating this study guide was to cover all of the topics that you will see on the test. We also strove to make our practice questions as similar as possible to what you will encounter on test day. With that being said, if you found something that you feel was not up to your standards, please send us an email and let us know.

We would also like to let you know about other books in our catalog that may interest you.

SAT Math 1

This can be found on Amazon: amazon.com/dp/1628454717

SAT Biology

amazon.com/dp/1628454806

SAT

amazon.com/dp/1628455217

ACCUPLACER

amazon.com/dp/162845492X

AP Biology

amazon.com/dp/1628454989

We have study guides in a wide variety of fields. If the one you are looking for isn't listed above, then try searching for it on Amazon or send us an email.

Thanks Again and Happy Testing!
Product Development Team
info@studyguideteam.com

Interested in buying more than 10 copies of our product? Contact us about bulk discounts:

bulkorders@studyguideteam.com

FREE Test Taking Tips DVD Offer

To help us better serve you, we have developed a Test Taking Tips DVD that we would like to give you for FREE. **This DVD covers world-class test taking tips that you can use to be even more successful when you are taking your test.**

All that we ask is that you email us your feedback about your study guide. Please let us know what you thought about it – whether that is good, bad or indifferent.

To get your **FREE Test Taking Tips DVD**, email freedvd@studyguideteam.com with "FREE DVD" in the subject line and the following information in the body of the email:

  a. The title of your study guide.

  b. Your product rating on a scale of 1-5, with 5 being the highest rating.

  c. Your feedback about the study guide. What did you think of it?

  d. Your full name and shipping address to send your free DVD.

If you have any questions or concerns, please don't hesitate to contact us at freedvd@studyguideteam.com.

Thanks again!

Made in the USA
Columbia, SC
11 March 2019